Contradiction Days

Contradiction Days

AN ARTIST ON THE
VERGE OF MOTHERHOOD

JoAnna Novak

CATAPULT  NEW YORK

This is a work of nonfiction. However, some names and identifying details of individuals have been changed to protect their privacy, correspondence has been shortened for clarity, and dialogue has been reconstructed from memory.

First Catapult edition: 2023

ISBN: 978-1-64622-076-2

Library of Congress Control Number: 2022951937

Jacket design by Lexi Earle
Book design by Laura Berry

Catapult
New York, NY
books.catapult.co

Printed in the United States of America

10 9 8 7 6 5 4 3 2 1

We are born as verbs rather than nouns.

—AGNES MARTIN, "What Is Real?"

It is healthier to be sentimental about babies
than about skeletons.

—JOHN BERGER, *Permanent Red*

Summer 2019

1.

AT THE END OF JUNE, SHORTLY before I left for Taos, I tried to forget the baby. I laid a hand on my belly and felt him squirm. At night, the baby was active, kicking my false ribs. The 3D ultrasound images rendered him a clay-green doll-boy: snub nose, one dimple, and ten tiny floating fingers. I removed my hand. I tried to forget connotations of the word *belly*—paunchy, fat (see: beer), embroiling hell (see: of the beast). I inched to the edge of the mattress. I tried to forget my husband snoring beside me, and our dog, Lucy, curled into herself like a walnut in its shell at the foot of the bed. I tried to forget the bathroom scale. I tried to forget the private browser tab open on my phone. (In a 1977 letter to the director of the Guggenheim, painter Agnes Martin writes from Albuquerque: "PS I have no phone. Very inconvenient but I can't stand the suddenness of it.") I tried to forget debt pay-off plans (and redacted debt pay-off plans) in the notebook I'd devoted to notes on Agnes Martin. I tried to forget I was lying in a blissfully comfortable bed.

Often, the material comforts I sought enraged me—they reminded me of comforts I couldn't buy (currently: comfort with a schismatic identity: woman-who-puts-writing-first-and-never-wants-kid and pregnant-body) or they reminded me of my bourgeois bent—an unstraightenable bent—and then I'd feel extra ashamed to own a blissfully comfortable bed. I considered Grace Paley's adage, "Keep a low overhead," and I adored cathedral ceilings. And this was not a bad night. I didn't need to forget killing myself would end the shame and rage. I didn't need to forget my dark nerve. I simply tried to forget I was a wife, a daughter, a sister, a friend, a professor—and soon to be a mother. I tried to forget I was a writer. I turned on my side and wedged a pillow between my thighs. I imagined vapors of ambition, attachment, envy, desire, rage, ego, intellect, and pride floating off my body, like the souls of cartoon weasels shot dead: an empty mind requires an empty body, requires an empty mind. I tingled with hope. I thought: *I'm going to Taos. I'm going to write where Agnes Martin painted.*

Which was also where Agnes Martin wrote. For months,

I'd been obsessed with a German-and-English edition of *Agnes Martin: Writings*. Like any good obsession, this obsession had grown all-consuming. I read like a desperate sinner, ready to be raptured. Only occasionally, it struck me: this was the absolute worst time to be obsessed with Agnes Martin.

My therapist said there were no *shoulds*. I balked. *Shoulds* are everywhere when you're pregnant. Trudging through the second trimester, I felt I *should* be obsessed with the hazy formation of eyelids and nostrils; with dodging fishy mercury and upping my iron; with layettes, burp cloths, rompers, and impossibly small socks. My bible should've been *What to Expect* or *Pregnancy 101*. Other mothers-to-be cared for all that; when I didn't, I felt negligent and odd, like a good bad student—capable vamping as defiant. I was sad for the part of me that would die if I cared about motherly things. I resented the time I wasted mourning that part of me. Then I would be buoyed by choice. I'd feel cocky and hot. I wasn't bound to *shoulds* that would make my "pregnancy journey" a glowy, Goopy, consumerist bonanza. I was bound to the essays and poems of one of the most important American artists of the twentieth century; an eleventh-hour Abstract Expressionist; a Canadian-born champion of the West; a prophet of New Mexico; who lived as a pauper (save luxury sports cars); who rejected ostentation and fame like she rejected sex and feminism and gender and distinctions; who once joked/didn't joke she wasn't a woman but a doorknob; whose career spanned five decades; whose paintings, in the reproductions I paged through—grids and bands and stripes, in a palette the color of a faded photograph—were rigid, and also dreamy.

Agnes Martin, as one critic put it on the occasion of the artist's 1992 retrospective at the Whitney, had attained cult status as homesteading heir to O'Keeffe's New Mexico, "a guru of female self-reliance." I hated that critic. I hated her dismissal of Martin's writings: "little sayings extolling her spartan ways." Also, it was wrong. *Agnes Martin: Writings* includes no extolments of her spartan ways—at least, not in detail. Martin doesn't write about her dietary tics: only walnuts and hard cheese and tomatoes one season; Knox gelatin with bananas another; a pot of soup simmering for days on end. She doesn't write about her prairie-born hardiness: her facility with a chainsaw, her ability to man a tractor or collect rainwater or build stretchers for her canvases or mold adobe bricks. She's more universal.

Like Teresa of Ávila, whose *Interior Castle* Martin admired, she writes about interior life: suffering, joy, beauty, perfection, vision, rooting her precepts in the existence of the artist. A poetics of creativity. She doesn't write "little sayings." She writes short, pragmatic paragraphs broken into verse, lines interrupted mid-clause, polished to a scriptural sheen. It didn't matter how many times I read the essays, their themes— eschewing ideas and the intellect for positive feelings; art born of happiness and innocence and beauty; tendering the virtues of solitude—entranced me. *Entrance*: a doorway or a gate, and to fill with wonder and delight, and to cast a spell on. When I read Agnes Martin, where do I go? What spell does she cast?

Perhaps a tundra of white space, where I can jam myself into her enjambments. Perhaps her high-desert solitude—the ideal state for the artist—is so alluring to me because achieving it is not only elusive and hard, but, carrying the baby, a biological impossibility. I had a predilection for impossibility. "You impose these totally unreasonable expectations on yourself," my husband would say. My husband was right. It was an unreasonable expectation—that I could go to Taos and live like Agnes Martin, pregnant, with a husband and a dog.

Trying to find the "unwritten page" that Martin looked for in her mind—a simple visualization—was my first test.

"If my mind was empty enough I could see it," Martin says of the unwritten page. Teaching, I always told students to be precise: a writer *writes* isn't the same as a writer *says*. But for Martin, says *is* the verb. "The Untroubled Mind" hadn't been *written* by Martin at all—another artist, Ann Wilson, had transcribed it from Martin's speech. Martin said, Wilson wrote.

The transcription took place in New Mexico in 1972, when Martin was sixty. She'd arrived four years earlier in a white Dodge pickup purchased in Detroit with NEA money, hauling a camper by the hitch. She bought the truck after abruptly leaving New York City in 1967, and she'd spent eighteen months driving around North America, camping alone in state and national parks until, called by inspiration to New Mexico, she'd leased fifty acres atop Portales mesa, twenty miles from Cuba, for ten dollars a month. Martin had lived in New Mexico earlier; in her thirties, she had taken art classes at the University of New Mexico in Albuquerque (1946); later, portrait and plein air landscape classes in the Summer Field School of Art in Taos. Forking red dirt roads, arroyos, pinyon forests, streams to wade. When she returned in 1968, first she lived in her truck, then the camper, after she'd "adobed it up," as Wilson put it. She built buildings on the land: a one-room house, a mushroom hut; later, a studio. She collected rainwater in a tub and dug a well. She skinned deer and cleaned bearskins for locals.

Wilson arrived armed with questions from Suzanne Delehanty, who was curating ICA Philadelphia's Agnes Martin retrospective, her largest show since leaving New York. Answering the questions, Martin spoke like the schoolteacher she'd once been, slowly, with great composure. Critics describe her speech with words like *cerebral, oracular, obfuscating, possessed, monotone, pronouncement, aphorism, falling into trances*— largely omitting the decided tenderness of her voice, how softly she spoke, how often she laughed.

Beyond that, I didn't have more to go on. I'd been reading the essay in Dieter Schwartz's German-and-English edition of Martin's writing. The book has a dove-gray cover, a stiff spine, and its low-gloss pages are yellowed at the edges. A few plates with images I'd glance over when I flipped to Contents. In this book, the Contents was at the end.

Outside our house, a cat yowled, and a freight train shrieked on the tracks. June had been a month of storms. Lightning veined the skylights; thunder shook the windows.

Perhaps it was better for finding the "unwritten page" that

I had not seen an Agnes Martin painting in person. In Taos I would see many. I liked the paintings in reproduction, especially those from the 1980s: her airy, cloud-soft palette, her sure, etcherly lines. I liked her vertical paintings, the grids that brought her fame at the Betty Parsons Gallery, canvases china-inked or gold-leafed. I even liked the early, figurative paintings—at least, what had escaped her bonfire: Miró-ish biomorphs she called "personages," a self-portrait, a female nude. Paging through reproductions, I'd wonder how it would feel to stand in front of her canvases. In reproduction, I found the art lovely, just not very moving, unless I imagined her at work.

I peered through the clerestory windows into her thirty-five-feet-by-thirty-five-feet studio on the mesa. The process begun, a vision or a voice, inspiration the size of a postage stamp in her mind. Until then, she works on the land or waits in bed. A vision she is tasked to scale. She calculates proportions on a sheet of paper, private math, a sprawl of numbers. It's quiet here, enclosed by logs she sawed herself. No electricity, no running water, no neighbor for miles. She stretches and double-gessoes her canvas. Six feet by six feet, big enough for the viewer to walk into. She stretches two strips of tape over the canvas. Inching with a child-size ruler and a graphite pencil, she follows the tape, marking the lines. They form bands or stripes, some narrow, some wide, always a balanced pattern. Harmony. She turns the painting on its side to paint between the lines, so the horizontal color won't run vertical. With a two-inch housepainter's brush, she works down and up, applying acrylics she waters down to washes, sand yellow, pond blue, carmine sheered pink. The brushstrokes dissolve. The color doesn't pool or drip. She can't introduce an error. The mind knows perfection; she knows within five minutes if the painting is any good. If it isn't, she'll destroy it. Do it all again.

I went to the bathroom, kept the lights off, and didn't look in the mirror. I got back in bed and resettled on my side. The ceiling fan raced, whipping the air. The fan was poorly mounted. A year later, it would whip itself off the spindle and crash down inches from where I was nursing my son. I'd scream and my son would hardly notice, lying in my arms, eyes gently shut, mouth focused. Now, I covered my head with the blanket, closed my eyes, and unclenched my jaw. I waited.

And there it was: tiny, triangular, white, a corner. As if peeling up a sheet of carbon paper, slowly my mind lifted away the dark.

2.

Taos wouldn't be our first trip to New Mexico. The winter before, driving between California and Illinois, my husband and I stopped in Santa Fe. The seven hours from Sedona had been relentlessly beautiful, the landscape repeating, zoetropic, brown, green, ice white. We hit Santa Fe at sunset and drove to the Plaza. "God's Plan" droned on the radio.

Our hotel was once an abbey; now it was romantic. I'd found it on Goop. I felt basic/penniless consulting Goop, but from the lobby it was obvious the suggestion was good: talc-white walls; dramatic beams; pillar candles smoldering before barefoot St. Francis, hunky in a mosaic grotto. After a whiskey and sage at the bar, I extended our stay.

The snow held off. The sky was shifting, tucking away the sun, Payne's gray with the promise of snow. We tugged an après-ski turtleneck on Lucy and walked around the city, all cobblestones and turquoise and adobe, through galleries of silver tongue sculptures and insipid desertscapes, into a Frito pie five-and-dime. At a tasting room we ordered a flight of New Mexico sparkling wine, *méthode champenoise*. We showered together, almost had sex, did not have sex. We were too drunk and hungry, or we'd had sex that morning in Sedona, and that was enough for twelve hours. All sex was important. On this trip, I told my husband to start coming inside me.

Now it was evening. I wore size 24 black jeans and black ankle boots, my chestnut brown coat with a line of black buttons hidden behind a pleat in the back. I felt irresistibly usable and beautiful. Drunk enough to feel thin enough.

Two-drinks drunk, decadent. Margaritas and Christmas-style enchiladas at The Shed. Three drinks, four. My heels clicked up the sidewalk and rapped up plank steps. We wandered into Shiprock, a second-floor gallery of Navajo tapestries. We looked at Italian cowboy boots and Moncler puffers light as cotton candy. We popped into a bookstore, bought the new Lucia Berlin; into a boutique, laughed at ugly knits; into a chocolate salon, marveled at so much red chile. Found a rooftop and drank frosty martinis with mole bitters.

After that, everything pretty much went downhill: I saw

myself leaving the tin-awninged bar, staggering toward a curve of stairs, throwing my body against a heavy door. Cold rushed into my ears. Alcohol singed my throat. I had the spins, and I was reaching for my husband's arm with my fingertips, looking for balance—when I jolted with repulsion: I should not have let myself get like this. Dumb needy bitch. I shoved my hands in my pockets and dug my nails into my palms.

Shut my eyes. Opened them. Squinted.

The cobblestones seemed very far away.

We got back to the hotel, and I erupted. Suddenly I was rude, vile, furious, and my heart was pounding. It had happened before and it terrified me afterward—these tirades that spiraled into despair, despair that spiraled back to rage, rage that led to a torturous urge to self-destruct. In the throes of these states, I couldn't remember that I would ever get out. There wasn't an *out*—and if there were, why would I be so naive to think it was worth trying to get out? What was the point? I was worthless. Garbage. Waste of resources, waste of energy, pathetic, I bled money, I ate and drank and ate and drank, acquisitive, shallow, fat-fucking-poseur piece of shit, acting like I was . . . Who? What? In a cramped room in a $$$$ hotel, in boots that cost more than the mortgage . . . *I* was the disgusting specimen trying to have a child? Another human deserved to be roped into *my* gross hedonism? If I could even get pregnant. If. I didn't deserve to. I didn't deserve anything. If I did get pregnant, I deserved the whole elimination of my life thus far.

"Fucking piece of shit," I screamed at my husband, hurling my boots across the room.

He ducked, held his hands in front of his chest, eyes frightened. Lucy cowered in her carrier.

"That's who you married—a fucking piece of shit. Go find another woman to have your child. Your dad hunts: tell him to gun me down before anything implants. I'm garbage."

Other machinations to this madness: I don't remember them. My speech bled into sobs, my sobs barked into wails. I was hideous. I remember stepping up into the bathroom with my husband, brushing my teeth, trying to calm down, starting to argue, starting to cry, trying to hold back sobs, my husband asking me where this was coming from, what was wrong, me yelling, searching for the boots I had thrown, telling him I was leaving, taking the car keys and sneaking down the service stairwell and pushing open a door.

I was on the side of the hotel, facing the dumpsters. There was our car, windshield shaved with frost. I ran the motor, windows up, blasting the heat, sobbing, frantic for a way this could kill me. I googled "suicide car running." I ignored my husband's calls for two hours; he must've contacted my family—I ignored my mother's calls, my sister's; those stopped; I gave up. I was too tired to die, too scared of death's abyss—in my thinking, the end of thinking. *Fucking coward*, I thought. Two hours after I left, I went back to the room.

The next morning, I was hungover and mortified at breakfast. I was another person.

"I'm sorry," I said to my husband. With my eyes, I tried

to convey great contrition. "That—that wasn't fair to you. It wasn't fair to my family. It wasn't fair to me. That—it was totally unacceptable."

The fork shook in my hands. I pricked the poached egg on my blue corn grits and watched the yolk bleed. My husband and I had been together fifteen years, and I still thought he didn't understand how bad my depression could get.

I was eighteen when I attempted suicide, twin aspirin overdoses, mid-August, late September; he met me several months later. During those college years, I often asked myself if he were the only thing holding me together. I didn't like the answer. When I went home on break, I'd fall into a familiar anorexia: Spinach salads, just leaves and turds of pre-crumbled goat cheese (easier to measure) drizzled with diet raspberry vinaigrette, sickly with Splenda and welt pink. Protein bars I coursed into a meal, scraping the chocolate-ish coating with my front teeth like a maniacal rabbit. Ninety minutes on the elliptical before bed; wake up to cramps in my calves; repeat. I was twenty-one when he left for grad school. *We* decided to "do" long distance, and *I* decided to lose ten pounds before his first visit. Even though he'd seen me ten pounds thinner, the new ten-pounds-thinner would impress him. It would impress me.

I'd always considered myself an "all or nothing" person. That fall I became an "all *and* nothing" person, starving myself witless until I binged on peanut butter from the jar or fun-size packs of candy corn or the edges of blondies I'd bake for lit mag meetings, then vomited—six or eight times a day, stopping only when the bile came out streaked with blood—then two hours on the treadmill (I couldn't eat there), listening to *FutureSex/LoveSounds* on my iPod because it was 2006. Finally, after two and a half months of this, I called my father and told him I needed to go to the hospital or I would die. I checked into inpatient treatment, almost a decade after my initial anorexia diagnosis.

That was the worst of it, I thought. That was many years ago.

At Pasqual's in Santa Fe, the dining room was homey and full. Outside, people snaked around the corner, waiting to eat. We were seated between couples, one in their thirties, like us, the other older. A pudding-faced manboy scrolled through his phone; his girlfriend fluffed her fox fur collar, stirred cream into her coffee, and photographed the mug. The other pair— retired professors, I guessed, by their fleece pillbox hats— sectioned out the paper. The calm ordinariness stung me. No one seemed to be repairing anything.

"You don't have to apologize to me," my husband said.

"That doesn't make it all right."

"I didn't say it's all right," he said. "I said you don't have to apologize."

We walked around the city, waiting for snow. We crossed a murmuring river. At SITE, we looked at raunchy dioramas. At the farmers market, we sampled honey and stroked lambswool throws. At St. Francis Cathedral Basilica, my eye caught an enormous gold case behind laureled bars. My husband went up to the altar and I knelt on the pew at the shrine.

Perched on a gilt pedestal was a tiny wooden woman. She

held a white-gowned baby the size of a peanut to her breast; a rosary spilled over her wrist. This was the oldest Madonna in the country: *La Conquistadora, Nuestra Señora del Rosario*, or Our Lady of Conquering Love.

In 1625, she was brought to Santa Fe by a Franciscan superior of the New Mexico missions, I read. The colonists worshipped her, dressing her like a Spanish queen. In 1680, the Pueblo people rebelled, killing twenty-one mission friars, and destroying the parish. The Virgin survived. Thirteen years later, Governor De Vargas announced his plan to retake Santa Fe under the Virgin's protection, "to rebuild her temple and throne." A year later, the parish began honoring her with an annual festival: novenas, processions, a shrine of boughs.

She represented, according to the pamphlet, "a phenomenon of love." What kind of love? A messy, contradictive love. Brutal, violent, murderous, colonizing, desperate, pious love. So much had been foisted on this doll. Still, looking at the Madonna, with her little lace mantilla and her golden crown and her scarlet moue, I asked for help. In her glassy gaze, my breakdown the previous night became a mere tantrum. She had survived four hundred years. Stravinsky had played in this nave; she'd traveled the world on a Marian tour. I felt sick with hope—that my outburst hadn't cursed my ability to conceive; that one day I wouldn't be so messed up; that I would be capable of calm, ordinary peace.

That afternoon, we drove out of town, up a mountain, ten thousand feet above sea level. We climbed two hundred steps to an outdoor Japanese bath.

We booked a tub suite for an hour. Time enough. We locked the gate. The tops of the pine trees peaked around us and beyond them the sun wavered, pallid in the sky. Large, invisible birds cawed. My husband untied my robe. There was a sauna, a hot tub with steam coming off it. The pepper of evergreens on the cold air, the cold plunge pool, its tight circle. Dropping in, going down a pipe or a chute—isn't that the best part of being fucked? The vanishing? Going under? There were two tiers of benches in the sauna. The spice of hot wood. First my husband laid me down on the lower bench and ate my pussy until I came. I had gold hoop earrings in: they burned the sides of my neck. Then I stood up, turned around, and leaned over the top bench, and he fucked me from behind. I bent over so that my elbows pressed into the wood, and every muscle in my upper arms engaged. I concentrated on the tension. My husband came quickly. He groaned. His semen trickled down my thigh. I staggered out of the sauna, shivering and sweaty, dizzy. It was forty degrees outside. The warmest part of the day. It still hadn't snowed.

We got into the hot tub. He kissed me, grabbed my neck, tugged my hair.

"Don't leave me," he said in my mouth. He pulled my body onto his. "Don't ever leave me."

————

Throughout the drive to Taos, my husband and I talked about Albuquerque. West, west, and more west—St. Louis, Bentonville, Oklahoma City, Amarillo—we joked about taking our son to the lavender farm and telling him he'd been conceived in the Sor Juana room. "Through hot sex," my husband added. I squinched up my face pretend-embarrassed, like a shy flirt, but of course I loved—was proud—the sex had been hot.

I was relieved he didn't mention Santa Fe. Even if he'd only brought up the good parts—sex at the springs, dinner at Geronimo—I still would've thought about the horrible night. The memory of it made me sick. Everything it foreshadowed.

But this time in New Mexico would be different. I would be different. I was on a quest. In 1993, Agnes Martin told Irving Sandler in *Art Monthly*, "You can't draw a perfect circle, but in your mind there is a perfect circle that you draw towards. You can't be a perfect man, but in your mind you can conceive of a perfect man." After all she'd endured, that she maintained this belief nearly brought me to tears.

Looking at her art tore me up in that way, too. Because it seemed so apparent that her paintings brushed up against perfection. And that's what I wanted. I wanted to write sentences as clearly, and as humanly, as Martin drew graphite lines across the canvas. I wanted to write sentences that emanated sublime beauty, like the thin belts of pale, pale red in *Desert Flower*. I wanted to write sentences that, in concert, achieved the grace and balance of her grids. I wanted all of it because I could sense the mind that had conceived of that delicate palette and those mathematically rational compositions, and that mind was like mine: it belonged to a person who had known profound turmoil. Who had borne incredible mental pain. I wanted to transform my own pain in that way, to make it abstracted, beautiful, oblique. I saw in Martin's painting everything I couldn't do in my writing.

Falling short agonized me. I searched for the problem. I'd had good schooling. I had a job teaching writing that let me think about craft. I had a writer husband who line-edited my drafts and laid manuscript pages on the floor with me, plotting out books. I had writer friends. I read rampantly. I wrote rampantly. I completed stories and poems and essays and novels. I sent out work. I published work. I kept lists of titles to use, lists of words to look up. I turned off my phone. I avoided television. I avoided podcasts. I woke up at 4:00 a.m. I stopped mid-run to write down a line. I woke mid-dream to scrawl a paragraph, two paragraphs, half an op-ed in my notebook. I kept a notebook. I didn't use social media. The more I searched, the more I feared the problem was internal. I was flawed. Maybe my appetite was the problem. Maybe my dependency on other people. Surely my arrogance and pride. Perhaps this is why Martin captivated me. She was humble and not humble. Her paintings were soft and exact. It seemed entirely possible that, by studying her, by trying to be like her, I could learn to tolerate my own contradictions—at least until motherhood upended everything.

While my husband drove past Angel Fire, I typed out the rules:

- No weighing
- No pitching articles

- No talking before writing
- No email
- No phone
- No thinking about how much food is or isn't enough
- No credit cards (live on cash—$16.70 per day—for eighteen days)
- Less speaking
- Less thinking about needing

If the trip had a theme, it was renunciation. I even renounced Martin—at least one line from "What Is Real?": "Do not settle for the experience of others." Because if you felt truly low, if you were bad in the worst way, if you'd reached your breaking point—couldn't there be an exception? Hadn't Martin done her share of mining the experience of others? *Pilgrim's Progress*, the Tao Te Ching, Gertrude Stein, and the Old Testament were known influences on Martin's prose. She could summon Bible passages: "indeed, the people are grass," from Isiah; Ezekiel's parable of the dry bones. When I read the parable, I copied a line from 37:13 in my notes: "Then you, my people, will know that I am the Lord, when I open your graves and bring you up from them." She had exhumed herself from the dirt. I needed to do that, too.

———

We drove into New Mexico on a drizzly Monday morning. The backseat was loaded with food: protein bars, kale chips, figlets, unsweetened coconut, oats, cacao nibs, chocolate chips (milk and semisweet), a gallon of olive oil, a half liter of balsamic vinegar, raspberry Emergen-C, cornmeal, cornstarch, cinnamon almond butter, six boxes of gluten-free spaghetti, four sweet potatoes, three yellow tins of anchovies, two onions, prenatal vitamins. Pantry remains. Rations for Taos Frugality. There was a dog carrier on the backseat, where Lucy stared out with black-rimmed eyes, head between her paws, and a scale I had slid in at the last second then vowed not to use, and a black backpack bulging with Agnes Martin books.

Except for *Writings*, they were hardcovers, the type of books I saw in museum shops and didn't buy. They'd arrived shrink-wrapped in plastic, dust-jacketed in vellum. Inside, the paper was heavy and cool. The image plates gleamed. One even included facsimiles of Martin's essay drafts, fragile sheets printed with her steno pad, her right-canting print. They'd cost a lot. I had purchased them with a small grant from the university where I taught—a grant that covered the casita in Taos, too—and even still, I was timid leafing through them. In my mind, I could conceive of the perfect response to her art—like the pure note of a copper bowl struck with a soft mallet—and I was terrified of falling short.

I needed to get over that. I was in Agnes Martin country now. For the next eighteen days, Martin could be my everything. I would read about her, write about her, and study her paintings at the Harwood Museum.

Nothing needed to interfere with this time. I'd applied for a grant to be free to do this work—so free, in fact, that

I might achieve the "positive freedom" Martin discusses in "What Is Real?" She had made her life a case study of positive freedom, giving up attachments to friends and lovers, jobs and politics, religion and possessions. I was doing that for less than three weeks.

You couldn't sever those attachments without a wound, or you didn't sever those attachments without having been wounded—if I had those thoughts, I pushed them aside. After all, being an artist necessitated a ruthless unconventionality— especially for women. In her 1971 essay, "Why Have There Been No Great Women Artists?" Linda Nochlin argues that, only by assuming "'masculine' attributes of single-mindedness, concentration, tenaciousness, and absorption in ideas and crafts-manship for their own sake," have women succeeded in art.

I was reading Martin's writing every day. And the more I read, the less I read *into* her. I was too caught up in the formula she hinted at: Simplicity = subtraction = sublimity. She reminded me of the fasting saints I'd idolized as a girl, women whose hunger made apparent the baseness of earthly desires and shepherded them toward God and salvation. Re-place God with inspiration, salvation with art.

Positive freedom, I hoped, would cure me of the negative feelings that held such power over my life. But more than that, I hoped positive freedom would make me a disciplined writer. It seemed to me that discipline, once achieved, would become permanent, encasing my identity as a writer in am-ber, where it would—hopefully—survive motherhood intact.

That writer friends often complimented my discipline,

that my discipline was born of ambition, that my ambition was for recognition and success, that recognition and success would satisfy my pride, I ignored. Discipline for discipline's sake was noble—lucky by-products or not. When I was young, my mother got the flu. She spoke giddily of the weight she'd lost as a result.

Only, I couldn't tell if I was renouncing too much or not enough. I struggled to talk about what Agnes Martin meant— let alone what she meant to me. At my baby shower, when asked about my summer plans, I'd mentioned the trip, saying I was going to research this painter who'd rejected the New York art world and lived monkishly in New Mexico, building her own house and painting these stunning paintings—hard to put into words—omitting specific details in an "I'm too deep in this study to explain it to you, Kind Relative Who Has Gifted Me *Chikka Chikka Boom Boom* Copy #2" way. At a folding table in my sister-in-law's living room, I said: "Off the grid." My husband's half cousin popped a peapod. I said: "Unplug." My flax-haired aunt chuckled, passing the Fuhgeddaboudit chicken. Everything came out half-baked, too digital-detox, too random. I sounded pretentious and false to myself; I assumed to others, too. If fetuses cringe, my son did.

I couldn't say I needed help. That meditating on Martin in Taos was my last grab for it. That, for many months, shit had been hard.

Open the grave. Bring me up.

———

In Carson National Forest, the evergreens shimmered through a fine veil of smoke. My husband drove. I loosened the seat belt over my belly. Lucy perched on my lap, peering out the window. I watched the map on my phone, the miles counting down toward Taos: 8.9, 8.8 . . .

"Do you smell that?" my husband said.

I sniffed, and Lucy did, too. I breathed in the echo of flames. The air was cabinly and warm, like flannel or toast. A pair of signs explained the situation: CONTROLLED BURN. DO NOT CALL. I took this as a good omen. The fire was contained. Earlier that day, we'd pulled off at a rest stop on the Ports-to-Plains Corridor to see New Mexico's largest extinct volcano, the Sierra Grande. Despite its distinctive elevation (8,720 feet), the volcano was pathetic, patchy and asparagus green. Still, I felt relieved: it was dormant. I hoped it would stay that way.

Now we were on Highway 64, riding through Cruz Canyon: 3.1, 3.0, 2.9. On one side of the road, a potter's studio in a wooden house on stilts. On the other, parking for trails. The casita we were renting was several miles from Taos Plaza. At a fork, we veered left. From Camino del Medio, we saw houses, large adobes, well distanced from one another or hidden behind iron gates. We turned. Not another car in sight. The road plowed into the desert.

3.

In front of the casita, I tipped my head back, overwhelmed by the field of puffy clouds in the vast blue sky. Then I hefted the fullest box from the car, the one with olive oil, vinegar, and potatoes.

"J," my husband said, "c'mon. Let me get that."

"I'm fine," I said.

He shook his head. "You know you're not supposed to lift stuff."

Behind my sunglasses, I rolled my eyes. I hated when he was protective, so vigilant about protocol. I'd feel reckless being a bare minimum of capable. Obviously, I'd think, he's only worried about the baby. But I also loved being watched, knowing he was looking at my body. From behind, *with my back to the world*—to take Martin entirely out of context—I didn't look pregnant. It was all aggravating and arousing, how he dad-ed me, eyeing my ass.

And, really, I *did* understand what I was and wasn't supposed to do. When I was six weeks pregnant, I'd gone running. The sky was wooly gray, fog-damp. On Twenty-Third Street, just south of downtown Los Angeles, the moisture in the air activated a stench: soggy cardboard, corn oil, coils of dog crap. I held my breath and dodged a Little Caesars box of puke. I jogged the first three blocks of my route, past Bonsallo, past the mural of sombrero-wearing skeletons on the lavender apartment building, campus, Estrella. I was slower than usual, aware of my belly with every stride.

Finally, I rounded the corner and halted in front of the charter school. It was a weekend. The building was locked up. Usually, the entryway swarmed with children in maroon and khaki, a couple clipboard adults. Now, I could hear their phantom chatter, their jabs of laughter, as they watched an old white lady check herself out in the mirrored doors. I turned sideways. Front. Sideways again. In profile, my lower abdomen bulged, barely, but still—it looked like I'd eaten an entire order of pad Thai or had a couple pillowcases stuffed in my hoodie's kangaroo pocket. I felt vain and slow. This was real. The pregnancy book sitting on our coffee table said: No jumping. No bouncing, jostling, jarring violent movements. I remembered a childhood friend's father, who used to call running "pounding your body against the pavement" (how extreme and violent and hot that sounded to me). Did the restriction apply to the first trimester or the second or the third? All of them? How much had I fucked up? I hadn't been running fast, and I was winded. That was bad. I slid my hand under my sweatshirt, above my waistband, onto my skin. I rubbed my stomach. I sulked for a moment, dejected not to be running. Then my disdain spread into terror, and I walked the rest of the three-mile loop. Had I already jostled the tiny embryonic cell mass? When I got home, I stood in the shower and dragged a bar of seaweed soap over my ribs. I rubbed the grit on my belly, whispering *hi baby hi baby hi baby hi baby.*

Our casita was one of five adobes on the property; at the north end of the gravel lot, a silver Airstream refracted the light. The Airstream was a good, Martinly sign. Out front, there was a hedged-in brick patio, with a set of wooden folding chairs and a table big enough for the *Writings.* Lucy ran around, sniffing rocks and roots and scrubby plants. Then she plopped down, paws long, like a Chihuahua-papillon sphinx. Tongue flapping, black lips peeled back in a manic smile, panting. The sun had come out.

As majestic as the landscape was, cradled by mountains and sky, inside the casita was modest. The primary living area consisted of a single room, with an ugly brown microsuede couch and a potbellied stove, a glass dining room table I would constantly bump into, and an island to articulate the kitchen. But one wall was floor-to-ceiling windows looking out on the backyard, everything in flagrant bloom: rangy wild bergamot with lavish heads of pale purple petals, louche scarlet fairy trumpets, and, close to the earth, foothill deer-weed with hairy leaves and pert yellow lips.

With the front door open, I listened to the muted surge of trucks; the mountains, flat and purple, emanating their Taos hum. You could practically hear the unwritten page.

We decided who would work where. My husband was as eager to be cut off from the world as I was. Like me, he'd turned off his phone. Like me, he had a writing project he wanted to get done. Like me, he wanted to manage the compulsions in his life. His aims, along with my urge to get close to Agnes Martin, filled me with anxiety. I didn't want to be in his way.

And yet on some level, I knew there was really nothing to worry about being in Taos with my husband. I was lucky. We were *a group of solitudes.*

I'd come upon that phrase in a footnote to a profile of Martin, something the artist Jack Youngerman had said to describe the clan of artists—including Martin and himself—who'd lived in the old sailmakers' lofts on lower Manhattan, Coenties Slip. Ellsworth Kelly, Robert Indiana, Lenore Tawney, Ann Wilson, everyone older (save Wilson), and serious. I was fascinated by that period in Martin's biography, 1957–1967. The developments in her art—she'd left behind circles and triangles for lines, long and horizontal, like combed strands of hair, or short and vertical, like tally marks. The diorama of her daily life: The enormous loft with those endless windows looking out onto the river, her pioneering domesticity—the blueberry muffins she made on a Sears acorn stove. Her legendary walkabouts, her daily chats with Kelly, the whispers of an attraction between her and Tawney. I knew nothing about Tawney before reading about Martin, and I still knew little. Only: Tawney was a textile artist, Tawney was beautiful, Tawney was a rich widow from Chicago, Tawney drove a red Bentley, Tawney paid for Martin's loft; Tawney looked at Martin's work and collected Martin's work (in one photo of Tawney's studio, you can see *The Laws*, Martin's 1958 assemblage: a nearly eight-foot-tall plank of salvaged wood painted two tones of blue—the bottom half, Normandy; the top, navy—studded with a grid of fifty salvaged boat spikes; beneath the spikes, a row of five unpainted squares show the naked wood). Martin looked at Tawney's weavings and wrote a statement for Tawney's 1961 show (one paragraph reads sim- ply: "There is penetration"); on occasion, they named each other's art. I got so caught up in the saga of creation—creating art, creating oneself, creating oneself as an artist—that I ig- nored the hardship of those years. Being a woman artist. Being a woman artist in the swaggering, post-Pollock days. Being older, being gay: Martin had come to New York when she was forty-five, on dealer Betty Parsons's dime. There was speculation that Parsons had been a lover, too. No, perhaps I only overlooked matters about which I felt ill-equipped to speak—say, life as a closeted queer person. Martin was never public about her relationships with women, refuted any cross- pollination between her and Tawney (to Joan Simon in 1995, on the influence of weaving on Martin's work, "Oh, don't give me that"). Speculating about her sexuality seemed not only a grave overstep, but a flattening of the person. An Annie Dillard line came to mind: "These things are not issues; they are mysteries." Still, I was keenly aware of the hardships that resonated with my own experience as a writer, that awful toggling between making and selling. Having a temperament that made you ill-suited to the whole business of art—networking, parties, alcohol—I had experience with that. Martin had had mental breakdowns in New York, multiple hospitalizations, months of amnesia after a trip to India, rounds of electroshock therapy. The way all of that drained you to the core. Later I'd come across a letter she'd sent to curator Samuel Wagstaff. In it, she writes of *Tundra* and *The Lake*, some of the last paintings she made before leaving New York, conceding that the work will have staying power, for she realizes now it was "conceived in purest melancholy."

My husband would take the bedroom at the front of the casita. This was where we'd sleep—big bed with rough sheets, love seat, rattan end tables shaped like timpani. I brought my things to the back room, which had filtered, aquarium light. I looked around. I felt charged up and good. This is where I'd work. I needed nothing more. There was a washer and dryer in one corner, a black table pushed against the wall, a bookshelf, and bunk beds.

One for her, I thought, one for me.

———

When I was a child, I loved an old series of books called *The Boxcar Children*. In my memory, there are four children, with parents who have been sent to war or labor camp, or perhaps the parents are dead. Whatever the cause of the absence, the parentlessness leads the children to make home in an abandoned boxcar. An elder sister plays momma, cozying the space, preparing beans and stew; a brother forages for furniture in rubbish heaps. I was enamored with the *world* of these novels—the word *setting*, all time and space, seemed to miss mood, that marvelous fourth dimension of fiction. Those autonomous, capable kids were my spirit siblings. I felt the thrill of not needing adults who were supposed to take care of you; I relished the scrappy, hectic energy of making do and repurposing trash, the way survival eliminated frivolous choice, the way life went on even if it were reduced to a rectangular box—the way, even, that life became more lovely and secure in a world of limited means.

I fantasized about a misfortune befalling me, forcing me to prove my ingenuity and pluck. (Perhaps my whole life, I've been fashioning such misfortunes.) On Hospitality Sundays after Mass, while my mom and dad and brother and sister were eating doughnut holes and drinking apple juice in the parish center, I'd steal away to the handicapped bathroom. It was a long, rectangular box. I'd stand there like an interior designer on TV, smartly, coolly, surveying the quarters. The fantasy of surviving on near nothing made me a shark. The toilet paper shelf? My few possessions—clothes, books, a mug (you wouldn't need a bowl if you had a mug)—would go there. A sleeping bag on the floor. A little table and a folding chair. Yes, yes, I could see it. All I needed fit in that box.

Setting up the back bedroom, I felt that same self-sufficiency, the promise of containment as a pleasure. Certain borders of existence. My therapist talked about anorexia as a disease of self-enclosure. I'm sure he didn't mean that to have a particular valence, but I was glad I was no longer sick—certainly not as sick as I'd once been—because the notion of self-enclosure—of being sealed off, un-needing—would've only enhanced anorexia's allure.

I knew I was still vulnerable to that allure because self-enclosure was what drew me to Martin. It was something I loved about her paintings. How the outside world is kept out—not a face, not a freckle, not an eye, not a mouth. Everything reduced to color and line, so orderly even her effort is invisible. Annette Michelson in 1967, reviewing Martin's recent paintings (the paintings conceived in "purest melancholy"), sees the work's "ultimate ineffability" as "determined by the rigor of its arithmetic rationale . . . one reaches for a tape measure, only to relinquish it, knowing that verification of that rationale will in no way account for the interest of the work."

I had to relinquish more than the tape measure (or the scale) when I looked at her art, especially shrunk in reproduction. I relinquished the need for voluble sense. It was a kind of thrilling gag, knowing I couldn't put into words my response to the work yet experiencing a diffuse, numbing release, like I'd been stuck with a shot of dopamine.

I kept coming back to a plate with *Milk River*. In person, the canvas would be seventy-two by seventy-two inches, nearly a foot taller than me. In reproduction I could see it was covered with a pasty coat of acrylic, ochre with an olive cast. Nine-tenths of the composition is consumed by a rectangle formed of slender, horizontal lines drawn in off-white colored pencil. The lines are angel-hair thin, so close together and subtle in their variation they seem to vibrate. Through them, the paint is barely visible; it appears like a flush spread up a lover's neck. If it weren't for the border, the color would be indeterminate.

You could think about process, about the punishing energy of repetition, the labor of drawing slender line after slender line. I suppose you could think about the title, its suggestion of mammary streams, rivulets of milk whizzing from a nipple. But I didn't think about any of that. Unlike pregnancy, where a smear of brie could mean birth defects, there was no consequence I felt pressured to worry from Martin's art. It felt sexy and naughty to be intimate with the work, not caring what it meant. Intimacy was the only value. I wanted to be alone with her.

4.

THE FIRST TIME I CAME IN MY
sleep, I was seven weeks pregnant.
I woke parched, breathing heavy,
lightly wondering if my husband had
eaten me out while I was unconscious.

I looked around the living room,
where we'd been sleeping. The bedroom in our apartment was too small
for a full mattress and a dresser. We'd
tried the bed against a wall or centered, and either I was climbing over
my husband, or he was crawling over
me or one of us was wedging past the
windowsill, straddling the corner,
squeezing by the dresser; once I'd
broken my pinky toe. I often wondered if other people gave up on the

conventional designations of their living spaces. Years ago, we'd shunted a sofa into a kitchen.

My husband was smiling peacefully in his sleep, cheek pressed to his strong, tan arm. Seeing his bicep made me want to wake him up, tell him about this bodily visitation, still reverberant. I wanted to take his hand and push his fingers into the slickness between my legs. I might come again if he touched me.

Instead, I kept private and inspired. The bed was directly in view through the front door. The door was all windows, a red-mullioned grid, sixteen panes of rectangular light. It thrilled me to know anyone could come up the stairs and knock on our front door, our landlord delivering a package, his adult daughter who liked to bring me cookies and tacos, anyone could see how ready my body was to seize and release.

There were no voyeurs, though. It was early when the orgasm woke me. I touched myself: still wet. I checked my stomach, and pretended it was still flat.

Soon, I started having dreams. I was not unaware of my dreams before becoming pregnant, and after, when the dreams were intense and regular, I began to believe I was dreaming whole-bodied, for the first time in my life.

"In dreams," John Berger writes, "separate, even contradictory, truths can be entwined. A thing may be two things at the same time. A table of food and a sledge. A hook and a beak." That first trimester, in waking life, every truth was a separate, antagonistic entity.

Awake, I saw every sky pink, clawed with palm trees.

Awake, I drank a decaf espresso. It tasted too rich, buttery, bitter. Awake, *nothing* tasted good. Awake, most of the symptoms were not bad—*so* not bad I felt guilty. I was nauseated. Averse to smells. Awake, my mind was a chaos of feelings—happy, excited, calm, contemplative, brave, confident, critical, apathetic, bothered, mad, pissy, insolent, aroused, disturbed—feelings so intense and bewildering and desultory it was difficult to keep my thoughts straight. I didn't tell myself, be gentle with yourself; this is a hormonal surge. I didn't tell myself, stop being so self-critical. I told myself, you're fucked. No more imagining pulling the plug on the professorship and the freelancing and the editing; no more imagining leaving my husband and Lucy, absconding from my family and friends; no more imagining draining my 401(k) and selling the purses I'd "invested in" in my twenties and taking the money and buying my own camper and vanishing into the woods to live on instant coffee and protein bars and give my life to my writing.

If I were cheerful and optimistic about the baby, I'd transgressed myself; if I were depressed and hostile, I was ungrateful. So I was eager to sleep. I hadn't been so eager to sleep since the summer I tried to commit suicide.

Denuded by dreams, I felt myself come alive. If I woke early, I forced myself to stay in bed, like an indolent princess. I had the distinct impression I was repossessing myself.

In the past, I'd transcribed dreams upon waking, a practice I judged positively, though where those transcriptions are, or what knowledge they brought me, is hard to say. If I found those records, I'd be struck by the common symbols, the light surrealism, the convoluted plots. I've always dreamt in mazes, like the snaky stories I envy others for writing.

I'm often ambivalent about contradictory aspects of myself. A fool for discipline, a greater fool for impulsivity. One thing is for certain: the pregnant dreams were always about sex.

————

Outside the casita, one bird questioned and another snickered. Otherwise, the back bedroom was quiet. I was reading over the notes I'd taken on Agnes Martin's life. Or trying to. The desk chair faced a wall. I looked around.

I was stuck on this detail: at Coenties Slip, Martin put a bathtub in the bedroom. I'd been trying to write, and I found myself writing about the bed in the living room, the couch in the kitchen. Did other people do these things? I tried not to exaggerate the significance of these coincidences. In fact, I'd been debating whether to mention my own history of competitive swimming—uncompetitive competitive swimming, from ages eleven to fourteen, wherein I was slow, lumbering, only good at no-breathers—or my own difficult mother: more I had in common with Martin.

It feels too messy, too sycophantic, too desperate to cite those shared traits. A little like a kid with a crush—she likes drawing and I like drawing?

Embarrassed, I tried to ground myself in the space. I planted my feet on the floor and felt the cool, glazed bricks.

There was a wooden sky, a ceiling of flat boards running

long ways, and six round vigas—practically tree trunks. I could feel the heat through the windows, even with the parchment shades down. The black-eyed Susans' shadows waved. When the wind picked up, their stems and petals blurred like frantic hands.

The room was sunken, with two doorways: you stepped down from the living area, walked though, and stepped up to open the door to the side yard, with the hammock. I liked being cupped. I liked having two ins, two outs. But mostly, I liked the bunk beds, their dorm-camp-barracks-sleepover vibes. They were dressed in bright covers, a turquoise and gold duvet featuring Kokopelli, the hunchbacked, streamer-haired fertility god of the Southwest. Kokopelli played his flute. On each bed, there was a pillow, perfect for raising one's hips. The pillowcase was patterned with two bow ties, touching.

At my desk, I tried to focus—on anything but the bed. There was one rule I hadn't written down: no porn. I couldn't tell if it was too shameful to put into writing, or if it was too obviously encompassed by the No Internet rule (in which case, why torture myself by putting it in writing?). Or, perhaps, I wasn't convinced that abstaining would benefit me. I wasn't even sure that being free of it would make me freer.

I hadn't watched porn much before I was pregnant, but the impending end of solitude led me to get myself off with more furtiveness and frequency than ever before. In the first trimester, when I couldn't work out hard or starve (I missed not eating more than wine), this was the private joy I found in pregnancy.

A message from my body to my brain: take this (and take this), this is yours.

The allure was not in being "bad," though this language often ran through the porn I sought. "You're a bad girl, aren't you?" "You're a naughty slut." "Give hole."

I didn't feel guilty watching porn, nor did I feel guilty for my tastes, nor did I feel guilty knowing the baby boy inside was, by corporeal osmosis, absorbing media that could be labeled misogynistic, exploitative, a product of heteronormative patriarchal capitalism, dehumanizing, vulgar, vile. Maybe my orgasm would make him happy—a little uterine massage. No, it felt important to protect this piece of myself, to hone it, honor it, hoard it, indulge it, when I gave the rest to him.

That night when I came in my sleep—what did I dream?

"Because I cannot see," writes Agnes Martin in "Staleness," "because I cannot know my desire."

That's the cop-out of porn—the way it convinces you you can see and know and categorically select your desire. And yet, that first trimester, God, the rush when I decided, alone in the apartment, that I needed to get off. Lying in bed or sitting in the living room or leaning against a wall. I turned the volume down on my computer, where a moment ago I had been working.

(I liked) the way my heart leapt typing "gangbang."

(I liked) my thoughts clouding and sharpening in the same instant, like plunging underwater, freezing and acclimating in a lurch.

(I liked) seeing how long I could watch a video. Two minutes, five. I didn't even need to rub or finger myself.

(I liked that I liked) a body rocked, smacked, choked, bruised, welted.

(I liked) the buckling stomach, the quivering asshole, the stretching of a vagina raw.

I saw a woman wearing a mask with a strap-on fuck another woman off, and I liked that, too, so much that I felt all right about becoming a mother.

It kept me feeling sort of game. Like, I wasn't going to degenerate into a prude or one of those desexed women who give up on their bodies. It also made me sort of disgusted, because after I watched porn—the woman who milked a bunch of cocks into a martini glass and drank the cum, which I'd watched in our hotel room in Bentonville, after my mind wandered reading the Martin biography—I felt abject and gross. But watching porn also made me want to have sex more often, and having sex was extra sensate and heightened and so good while I was pregnant, and, again, I'd heard about women for whom sex is never the same after giving birth. One friend used the phrase *vagina blowout*. Selecting pornography where one woman endured a battery of penetration or where one woman endured an act of extreme incorporation or where one woman played the role of sexual stuntman—scenarios I found more appalling than arousing—was a game of fort-da I played with myself, meting out the *unlust* and discomfort, reeling myself back with unfettered arousal. What could I tolerate? As Freud writes:

"the unpleasurable nature of an experience does not always unsuit it for play."

My husband was out for a run. I was sitting on a black swivel chair with one caster missing. Every time I shifted my weight, the metal foot clunked. I tried to stay still. If I wasn't going to watch porn, I wanted to be running. When I thought about running, I thought about having a body. When I thought about having a body, I thought about having my own body. Feeling fast and lean. And that was truly torture. To keep my mind busy, I went over everything I recalled from the biography of Martin.

————

"I can remember the minute I was born," Martin told an interviewer. "I thought I was a small figure with a little sword and I was very happy. I thought I would cut my way through victory after victory. Then, they carried me into my mother and half my victories fell to the ground."

Those victories fell on March 22, 1912. This, I'd read, was the same year New Mexico became a state, Jackson Pollock was born, and the *Titanic* sank.

She was born in the Saskatchewan prairie town of Macklin, on many acres of farmland, the third of four children. She had two brothers and a sister. Her father, a wheat farmer, died when she was two; she was close to her maternal grandfather; her mother detested her.

She remembered her mother as strict and abusive. She remembered her locking her out on the porch when she was two, her mother loading her on a trolley alone to get her tonsils removed when she was six. She believed her mother resented her for interfering with her social life. And yet, in interviews, Martin also said she was a good mother, that she'd learned discipline from her. Her mother came from means, and she worked hard to maintain a certain standard of living. By the time Agnes was seven, Margaret Martin had moved the family to Vancouver, where her own father lived. There, she bought, renovated, and furnished houses to bring in money.

Other things: Martin felt smarter than her sister, Maribel. She drew and copied pictures of famous paintings with her brother, Malcolm. In one photo from childhood, her hair is very short, parted to the side in a pageboy; she holds a cat.

Notes about being promiscuous in high school. Notes about being "[nastily teased.]" I wondered if the fooling around had been more sinister, if the teasing had been worse than nasty. Because a few years after graduating from high school in Vancouver, she moved to Bellingham, Washington, to live with her sister, where she redid high school.

Somewhere, I read she helped her sister through a pregnancy; somewhere else, I read she helped her sister through an illness. But who is healing whom after that bullying?

(Fleeting fantasy where I play her sister.)

For a while, she went back and forth between the States and Canada. A competitive swimmer, she placed fourth in the 1928 Olympic trials. Throughout her life, she swam, eventually donating a municipal pool to the city of Taos. (I'd break my internet rules to look for that pool and never find it.)

There's something briefly satisfying about solving a riddle. For a taste of satisfaction, trace her mature iconography to any of it: the flat, expansive prairie stitched with railroad ties; sheets of newsprint lined with rows of lined guides for practice cursive; rows of pews in a Macklin church; aqueous blue pool water corded with lane lines.

She was in her twenties. The jobs and the schools and the jobs at schools start to get tangled. She graduated from junior college at Washington State Normal School with a teaching certificate. Or first there was a California semester, class at UCLA or USC, chauffeuring for a young John Huston! Agnes in the world. She would bake pies at a bakery, teach first grade, work in a one-room schoolhouse, work as a lumberyard cook, operate an elevator in a boys' school.

For many years, traveling the continent, she was always around children.

She began studying at Columbia Teachers College in 1942 and would return to complete the degree in 1952, obtaining an MA in education with an emphasis in fine arts. During her second stint, she could've attended D. T. Suzuki's lectures, along with artists and intellectuals like John Cage. In between, she went to New Mexico and took classes at the University of Albuquerque, at the Summer Field School in Taos. More instructing children. In one unit, she taught them to build simple, habitable structures. A year later, she was a dorm mother for boys at a juvenile delinquent center.

After returning to New York and completing her MA,

Martin settled in Taos. This was the moment of being called; of self-sacrifice in the name of a higher power (art); a moment I loved: "I decided I would paint even if I starved," she told Benita Eisler.

For a while, she lived in a chicken coop—at least, a room the size of a chicken coop. No heat, no indoor plumbing. Actually, it was a dirt-floor shed, with a fireplace and a rocking chair, the only art an abstract canvas of a black oculus, a black whirlpool. (Why do I insist on two descriptions when one will do? And why do I write *whirlpool*, Hollywood symbol of the day for gushing, voiding (female) madness. *Associated with certain forms of hysteria.* Don't I trust myself to convey it well enough in one term, one life?)

In one picture from the shed, she holds two brushes in her right hand, one in her left. She wears a square-necked black shirt and an apron. She's always wearing an apron over her clothes, the smockish pinny sort, a garment both protective and decorative. Aproned, you're costumed in plain sight. You don an apron when you might make a mess of your clothes. When you need to protect yourself. To illustrate servitude. The apron suggests cook, artist, welder, bishop, sexy French maid. In medical parlance, an apron denotes a fold of stomach fat obscuring the genital region; in song, *sugar pie honey bunch*, the besotted is tied to the beloved's apron strings, too much under her sway.

Same room, different shot, different angle: She stands in front of a stack of canvases, this time in a railroad-striped smock. In this desert, years recede into mountains. She is forty-two or thirty-six, riding past the old ranchos to deliver messages to families of servicemen.

There's another photo of her from those days, posing on horseback in front of a shaky wire fence. The horse looks bemused. Martin's jeans cuff her ankles; she wears a blousy white button-down; her hair is swept into a Gibson girl bun.

She had Gibson girl pinups in the mesa. But I'm getting ahead of myself.

When she returned to Taos, her art was in flux. Not much of it remains. *Auto-destruction* is the term used to refer to artists' destroying their own work. (An idea for a poem: catalog and describe everything she burned.) Gradually, her work became less pictorial, less representational, less interested in recognizable earthly delights. Watercolor landscapes gave way to shapes, vaporous scenes, personages, forms: lozenge, bumper, areola. I was especially curious about a blurry Cubist expulsion from the garden—in New York, Martin would read Alban's *The Lives of Saints* with Lenore Tawney and study Teresa of Ávila.

But first she was discovered. And to be discovered, she was not without ambition, and to have ambition, one surely has ego. Despite the Protestant work ethic, despite her writing, despite her shared ethos with Ellsworth Kelly (to remove the self from art)—as David Witt writes in *Modernists in Taos*: "None of the other Taos artists then seemed to experience the overwhelming drive to become famous." She received a grant from the Wurlitzer Foundation, then the invitation from Betty Parsons.

I'd only finished reading the biography in Amarillo, but two days later already so much was hazy.

I remembered that Betty Parsons moved her to New York; I remembered that Parsons came from a wealthy family, that Parsons was a lesbian; I remembered that Parsons wasn't great about paying her artists or that Parsons charged artists. I couldn't remember if Martin moved from Parsons to Castelli or Parsons to Elkon (Elkon). I couldn't remember the year of her first MoMA show (1965, *The Responsive Eye*). I couldn't remember the first year she showed grids (1961). I couldn't remember the name of the year of the Minimalist show (*10*, at the Dwan Gallery, in 1966; Martin was decidedly not a Minimalist, though in 1976, she told John Gruen: "It's possible to regret that you're not something else").

I regretted that all I really remembered were the lofts; the muffins; the camaraderie. I remembered a photo of Martin and Kelly capering on bicycles. I remembered a picture of Tawney's beautiful studio, the loom, the weavings hung from the ceiling. I remembered Martin walking across the Brooklyn Bridge (the best thing to do after finishing a painting, she'd said), Martin walking all over Manhattan. I remembered, maybe incorrectly, Martin having lunch with Rothko. Certainly respecting Rothko. I remembered at parties Martin would get drunk and give people personality tests, or lead them in weird visualization exercises, or recite Gertrude

Stein's "Lifting Belly." I remembered critics comparing her appearance to Stein's.

But that resemblance comes later. When she moved to New York, she was forty-five and striking, with limpid blue eyes and a soft mouth. Her hair was dark and long. In one photo, she faces a canvas in those quilted worker's jumpsuits she wore, a thick braid down her back. In another, she sits on the slope of a rooftop with the Coenties crew. The buildings of lower Manhattan tower and jut in the background, but there's this homey, Bohemian scene: Youngerman; his toddler, Duncan; his wife, Delphine; Indiana; Ellsworth. And off to the right, at the edge of the frame, at the edge of the roof, Agnes: legs long, ankles crossed, tennis shoes, hands in the pockets of her trench coat, hair in a low ponytail, smiling.

I loved that photograph—how alive and nurtured everyone looks.

Right, nurtured: Martin was maternal. Someone called her an earth mother, someone else called her a healer; Ann Wilson called her a mother in art. Someone said she makes you feel better, she soothes you, talking to her will help you when you've been out of sorts.

Also, she knew "the purest melancholy." And days of wandering around the city, her own name chewed away by confusion, a sustained amnesic trance, madness—no identification, lost on the streets, dirty, confused, committed to Bellevue. One hundred rounds of electroconvulsive therapy. A breakdown on a steamer in India.

And then it was 1967. "Every day I suddenly felt I wanted

to die," she later said. She was fifty-five. Gossip says a relationship fizzled (with the artist Chryssa). Her loft on 28
South Street was set for demolition. Her mentor, Ad Rein-
hardt, died of a massive heart attack on August 30. Within a
week, she had left the city, burning her paintings and giving
away her art supplies to younger artists, leaving New York so
abruptly friends didn't know she was gone.

And then the long road trip that ended in New Mexico,
on the mesa.

And then a trip to Germany in 1972 to make a series of
prints, *On a Clear Day.*

And then the ICA show in 1973.

And then she began painting again.

And then she left Elkon and signed with Pace Gallery,
where she stayed for the rest of her life.

And then, in 1976, she made a movie called *Gabriel*, about
a little boy exploring nature by himself, having a perfect day.
And then an idea to make a movie about Genghis Khan,
called *Captivity.*

And then she decided it wasn't natural to live outside
society.

And moved to Galisteo.

And moved to Taos.

And her paintings grew more beautiful.

Soft, with edges.

And she had plenty of money now, and she enjoyed
traveling, and she took cruises, and her psychiatrist adjusted her medication, and one year was a hard year, and

one year was an especially productive year, and she likened herself to a chicken, rising with the sun and going to bed before dark, often foregoing dinner. And she sat in a rocking chair in the gallery in the Harwood, watching her work being hung. And she spent the last twelve years of her life in a retirement home in Taos, where she painted in her studio every morning for three hours and lunched at the Trading Post Café with friends and spent afternoons reading (nothing that "sticks to your mind, preys upon you"), meditating twenty minutes twice a day, living her quiet life when she wasn't receiving the Golden Lion at the Venice Biennale in 1997, the National Medal of Honor from the Clintons in 1998. She died of congestive heart failure on December 16, 2004, at the age of ninety-two, and her last work was a contour drawing of a potted plant.

That is almost everything I knew.

———

Late that afternoon, my husband and I drove out to the Rio Grande Gorge Bridge after making love. The half-life thrum inside my vagina, his tongue, his fingers, his cock—my body plumb, stunned, aglow. The mountains. Sweeping pastels. Adobe houses, average barns, mansions, red and silver and blue roofs, valley-scattered, field-flung, everything a swath of horizontal color.

Making love is more horizontal than fucking. A bridge between people.

We parked on gravel, with other cars bound for the gorge.

We walked the shoulder, me, my husband, Lucy. The baby, too, here on our first full day in Taos.

Soon we came to a sidewalk. An interruption in the endless landscape. The sidewalk and a railing, metal the color of scalded milk. We were on a bridge overlooking the Rio Grande. I looked for signage revealing the distance down. Every ten feet there were call boxes to connect dialer with crisis line, stenciled: *There Is Hope*.

I did not want to die at this moment, so the message seemed hokey yet true. It was the afternoon before our wedding anniversary. I felt ashamed for the days these last months.

Now it was just layers of contentment: having arrived, having taken notes in my notebook and notes in my phone, having orgasmed, having a plan.

I would spend my working hours writing six-by-six-inch text blocks in tribute to Agnes Martin's signature canvas. It was not the first time I had fit myself into another woman. Growing up, I would search for a celebrity's weight and calculate how much Audrey Hepburn would weigh if she were my height. I'd always been horrible at proportions, and yet when I had resolve, I would shrink Audrey four inches. But I needed to stop seeing anorexia everywhere.

I was here to be like Agnes Martin, not relapse into the past.

I stared at the Rio. How did Martin look at this water?

My obviousness annoyed me. Or was it Martin's sibylline schtick? No. Another rule: I could not be suspicious of Martin when it was time to become Martin.

Ahead of us, the sky was faded, a durable uniform blue.

"Did you see the lightning?" my husband asked.

I shook my head. "No."

He'd seen lightning that morning, too, outside Angel Fire. Why was I always missing it, I wondered. Had the baby seen the lightning? Did he sense the current of electricity, the immensity of the river, my vertigo? I leaned over the railing. On this sidewalk, you were on a bridge. It seemed solid, but the bridge snuck up on you—no suspension, no ascent: it was under you, vibrating with the hunger of the gorge.

"There it is again," my husband said, pointing to the sky. "It's close."

I pretended not to hear. I looked down. Plants grew out of the cliffs, brindled, green, masking the steepness of the plunge. The Rio sloshed, the color of mud.

5.

"ARE YOU LOOKING FORWARD to going to the Harwood?" my husband asked. "To finally seeing an Agnes Martin in person?"

We were at the glass table, eating spaghetti slick with rust-dark chili oil. Day one had been a success: I'd stayed off the internet, stayed off my phone, left the scale in the trunk of the car, paid cash for the pecorino and kale, and wine.

I took a sip of wine. Wine was okay, half a glass, on occasion.

I was avoiding the questions.

South of the Plaza, a few blocks down Ledoux Street, in a sprawling two-story Pueblo revival—adobe with brilliant turquoise doors and window frames, squared-off archways that led into enchanting loggia—the Harwood housed many of Agnes Martin's paintings. We'd driven past the museum two hours earlier, returning to the casita. Yet, despite all I'd read and how far we'd traveled, I was afraid seeing her paintings would not change me. I was afraid seeing her paintings—twenty-five weeks pregnant, the baby kicking like a midfielder—would make it crushingly obvious that I hadn't done anything to move toward living a solitudinous life devoted to making art. I'd chosen the opposite for myself.

"I need to reset," I said carefully. "I need to take time to be fully immersed. Would you pass the pepper?"

How impossible it is to be fully here—present in the present—when you're pregnant. Pregnant, the present zips you between future and past: last period, last kick, next milestone of development (eyelashes), next appointment with ob-gyn (three weeks), due date (October 4). I didn't want to see things like that. I didn't want to see like a pregnant woman.

I wanted to see like Martin. If not like Martin, at least like an artist. In 1972, the year Martin dictated "The Untroubled Mind" to Ann Wilson, John Berger's four-part *Ways of Seeing* aired on the BBC, changing how a TV-watching public understood the image. Berger, a polymathic Leftist art critic and sui generis writer, had trained as an artist (his books incorporated documentary photos, later his own drawings). In *Ways of Seeing*, he translated his deep knowledge of the visual into roving, generous seminars, punctuated by close readings of paintings in museums and adverts in the tube, sharing circles with feminists and schoolchildren, and steadying sound bites: "In paintings, there is no unfolding time."

(Or as Martin once wrote: "I wish the idea of time would drain out of my cells.")

"Besides," I said to my husband. "They're closed on Tuesdays."

———

Once, nearly ten years earlier, my husband and I shared rugelach with a serious and famous writer. Offhandedly, the serious and famous writer mentioned she'd eaten a cheese sandwich for dinner. A cheese sandwich requires minimal effort. Bread and cheese cold from the fridge. Bread from a bag, cheese peeled from between sheets of deli paper. No knife. No cutting board. A late cheese sandwich when writing stretches into evening and evening stretches into night. The serious and famous writer said, I believe, that she *had* a cheese sandwich, rather than she *ate* a cheese sandwich—the verb a bruised maraschino on top of the whole downplaying sundae. Corporeal appetite relegated to a real dud of a word: *had*. There are no dud words when the serious and famous writer eats a cheese sandwich in her book-lined office. I imagine her working at dusk, pausing her pencil, the pink nub of the eraser the brightest object in the room. She must consume the sandwich, and I suppose she does so in one of two ways: rapidly, in seven or eight bites, to minimize the interruption to her work; or absentmindedly, taking a bite here, a bite there, nibbling evening into night. She must consume the sandwich—perhaps with a glass of milk or a cup of tea—and yet I can't see her chewing, swallowing, wiping her lips with a napkin. I see her hunched over her desk, the dictionary stand behind her, another dictionary at hand; beside her notepad, a plate with crumbs, triangular flecks of orange cheese, oat dust from seven-grain bread. A polylingual, MacArthur Genius mouse.

In an essay about his visit to Martin's studio on the mesa in 1974, Arne Glimcher, founder of Pace Gallery (and, at the time, her new dealer), cast food as a needless bother to the artist. "Not even the decision of planning a meal was allowed to distract her from the making of her paintings," he wrote. "To avoid a break in concentration, she ate the same thing every day."

My alarm went off at 4:00 a.m. I shut it off. My husband didn't move. In the dark, I pulled on a T-shirt, sweatpants, and a black angora sweater I'd laid out on the nightstand before bed. Barefoot, I walked around the bed and went out into the living room. I closed the door softly behind me.

There was a gurgle and puff in the kitchen. The coffee had brewed on its program. I flicked on the light by the sink and opened cabinets. The casita had a new set of everything. Everything matched. Everything made sense. I poured coffee into a squarish mug—one cup of regular was okay. I chewed two calciums. I went to the back room without turning on the lights (no break in concentration).

I opened my computer.

I was beginning.

I reminded myself how to draw a text box. For most of

her life, Martin had painted on six-by-six-feet square canvases. I'd follow her lead. Write within regular parameters.
I watched the rulers on the side and the top of the screen,
expanding the box until it was six inches wide and six inches
tall. I copied that box. I pressed "insert break," and pasted it
on a fresh page sixty times. I would be happy if I wrote sixty
text boxes on Martin while I was in Taos.

Then, I watched my cursor blink.

I didn't know what to say about Martin.

I closed my eyes. I opened them.

Here was my unwritten page.

On the way back from the gorge, I'd run into Cid's, the
big organic grocery. In the checkout lane, while the man
ahead of me paid for cashews and beef, I scanned faces. Had
anyone known Martin? Could they tell I was here for her?
My face felt rictal and tense. I needed to stop looking so hard.
"Free and easy wandering"—that's what Martin called the
ideal state for the artist.

I started typing. If these first text boxes amounted to "free
and easy wandering," all the better. Freely, easily, I wandered
through my memory. A six-by-six-inch square text box fills
up quickly, I found. I sipped coffee. I pushed up one arm
of the sweater and scratched my wrist. I wrote another. My
stomach growled.

I am hungry, I thought (break in concentration). No, keep
going (break in concentration). What time is it? (break). I
retrieved the menu bar clock, which typically I kept hidden (break). Ninety minutes had passed. I leaned back in the

swivel chair (break). It clunked loudly in the silence (break). I eyed my stomach in the dim blue light from the screen. It was the stomach I'd hated for twenty years.

No. Now it was a belly.

———

When I found out I was pregnant, I revolted. A brief period of indulgence, a spree of bad feeding, a whatever of appetite, a fuck it of the mind, it tastes good, and I want it, let me hold it, touch it, smell it, tequila shots so close to my lips I tasted alcohol in my nose, hot in the back of my throat. Cake for breakfast, chocolate for breakfast, gummy vitamins, noodles for lunch, pizza dinners, caloric beverages; following pregnancy rules, abusing my own system, contradiction days: skipping lunch, ice cream after Thai, frozen yogurt; rice bowls blissed with caramelized pork head, blowing money on takeout, no arguing with a pregnant bitch.

Quick freight of weight in my hips and thighs, five pounds in ten days: horror.

The first ob-gyn I saw: thigh gap articulated in skinny corduroys, four gold rings, model-tall with a model's lank ponytail. Even my hair was fat next to Jennifer R., rotating staff at this office of Cedars-Sinai. I'd never meet her again.

"Am I gaining too fast?" I asked, avoiding my husband's eyes.

"Not at all." She peered at a screen, crossing her wishbone legs. "You're starting underweight."

My husband would repeat this information for months. I

knew better. I knew BMIs, height-weight charts, LA bodies, skinny-girl lies.

"No, really," I said, shrugging, like, c'mon be real with me. "Should I work out more?"

How would this continue for the next eight months?

Sometimes, I felt a vague contentment. The anticipation of a new purpose illustrated the tedium of everything else: writing, reading, teaching. Sometimes, I thought about holding the baby (I couldn't imagine how small), caring for the baby (I couldn't imagine the sweet milky smell), loving the baby (I couldn't imagine swaddling him, standing with him, swaying with him). On phone calls with family and friends, I enjoyed saying nothing. This secret felt divine and absurd.

Part of me was happy.

Yet when my husband and I shared the news (speakerphone to his mom: joyful tears; speakerphone to mine: "holy fuck"), I knew there was something I couldn't tell anyone.

I was terrified. I hated my body, I hated my pregnant body, and my body was only going to get more pregnant. And what about "pregnancy brain"? *Pregnancy 411* insisted it was, yes, a real thing, and totally worth giving yourself a break about.

My husband was excited, our families were excited, our friends were excited—*I* was excited. How could I also be so afraid? But I was consumed by fear: the hot-cold sniveling fear that my work, the restraint of discipline, would vanish. That I would disappear.

Frequently, I lied. I told my friends I was feeling amazing.

I told my family I was ecstatic. I told my husband I'd stopped caring how I ate. I told no one I was sustaining myself on fantasies. At night, driving back from frozen yogurt, I'd stare at the headlights on the 10, blaring red and white across six lines of eastbound traffic, or gaze off, beyond the guardrails, into the sickled silhouettes of palm trees. Rats nested there, I'd heard. Tongue sugar-sour, thwarted energy pooled in my legs, I'd flick the door handle, imagining my body tumbling out, a soft terrible thud as I slammed into the road, caught under tires, and was crushed in an instant. One idea quieted my mind: I'd give birth and starve.

———

In the fridge there were protein bars. In the kitchen, I looked around. The bedroom door was closed. Lucy's dishes sat on the red floor. I refreshed her water. I refilled my coffee. There was a window over the sink. A film shimmered over the tall grasses outside, the hazy blanch of the sun.

I opened the fridge. Yogurt, fresh figs, walnuts, honey. I opened the cupboard and scanned the countertop. Almond butter, banana—not ripe. Pantry. Oatmeal?

Several years later, I was surprised to discover Martin had commented on her own weight. In an interview in 2001, she says sixty-four was the age when she let herself go. Now she was fat, she admitted, but if she were younger, she would change that. "I really think we get everything we want, and so if you don't want to get fat, just keep saying I want to be slender. . . I think it's terrible to be fat."

I envied Martin and the serious and famous writer, people whose titanic obedience—to painting or translation—stanched the fickle flow of hunger. I'd envied people like this since I was twelve, when I learned how much effort it took to not eat. Anger grew from that envy: I remembered standing by the trash bin in the choir room, where I spent lunch, saving the salami from a sandwich with mustard and Velveeta, balling up the bread and the cheese, mutilating the food before I tossed it. I resented appetiteless people so much that even writing nonfiction about anorexia, when it would've been easy—and flattering—to fudge the narrative and fashion myself into a champion faster, I did not.

Even oatmeal was complicated. I measured oats in a measuring cup and remeasured with the food scale. I pinched Maldon salt into the almond milk in the pot, and I thought, this salt is too nice for the circumstances. I peeled foil off a jar of almond butter and portioned it into the roiling oats. I sampled the almond butter plain, oats now oatmeal, oatmeal from pot to mug, more salt, back to desk, tasting, getting up, back to kitchen. Drizzled honey over the top. Zeroed the scale.

Back at my desk, I jammed a spoon into the oatmeal. It squelched. I pushed it aside and pulled down a book. I turned until I found the images.

On my desk was a two-page photographic spread—a preview of what awaited me, 3.3 miles away. Inside the Harwood was an octagonal room constructed in 1993 to permanently display Martin's work. This was the Agnes Martin Gallery.

I'd read about the gallery. Martin was consulted on its

design, and she liked to stop by and sit on one of the four Donald Judd benches she'd picked for the space, backless wooden cubes painted the yellow of 1960s traffic lights centered beneath an oculus, facing her seven paintings. I'd seen pictures of those, too. Now I looked at them again. Because the photograph showed the entire gallery, the paintings' scale translated, even if the hues did not. She completed them in 1993–1994, a study of horizontal lines, in gradations of pale yellow and baby-boy blue. Acrylic on linen, five feet by five feet (the dimensions she could manage in her eighties).

Sitting at that desk, I thought of what Martin had often repeated about the size of her paintings—how she wanted people to be able to step inside the work. And yet, it seemed to me that she hadn't wanted people to vanish into the image all alone. Though the paintings in the gallery were all untitled, they all had subtitles, as if she hadn't entirely settled on leaving the response entirely up to the viewer.

> *Untitled (Lovely Life)*
> *Untitled (Friendship)*
> *Untitled (Innocence)*
> *Untitled (Perfect Day)*
> *Untitled (Playing)*
> *Untitled (Ordinary Happiness)*
> *Untitled (Love)*

If the color palette weren't enough to direct viewers' emotional response, the titles surely finished the job. Martin the teacher, Martin the lecturer—her reluctance to do away with titles made sense. When I taught, I often told students titles were an opportunity for the writer to have their say, a space unencumbered by the persona of the narrator or the speaker. Titles were valuable. They were your instructions to the reader.

6.

I WAS WRITING IN THE BACK ROOM when there was a chuff. I glanced at my notes.

"You won't find the answers out there," Martin says in a May 1978 interview.

There was another chuff.

I looked over at the kidney-red bricks. Lucy's nose was pressed into the gap below the door. I heard her feathery tail sweeping the living room floor.

Not even pets, Martin cautioned. Pets prevented a "quiet state of mind."

I jotted questions into my text box.

Was the quiet state of mind inspiration or asylum?

Was money quiet?

(Having it: quiet state; wanting it: not.)

Was fizzy water allowed?

Was a pause to scratch the dog's belly quiet?

Could a quiet state include a lover, a child? If one were quieter to compensate?

Another chuff. Technically, it was my husband's time. We had agreed not to speak until noon. We'd divide the day with Lucy: he would take her in the morning, I would take her after lunch. Yesterday, I had her in the hammock while I read about the brain. I'd learned about Salpêtrière, the large psychiatric hospital in Paris, where Philippe Pinel, father of psychiatry, freed the committed from manacles and shackles.

I got up. Having a plan with my husband irritated me, even though I fetishized plans of my own. I opened the door. Lucy trotted down the stairs, past my desk, past the bunk beds, and up the step to the side door. She looked at me. I let her out.

Outside, the air was oily with woodsmoke. I stood on the walkway of trapezoidal stones, cold through my socks. There was scrub and grass, argent weedy things, a red-pom-pommed shrub. I had taken notes on what I'd read in the hammock and at the picnic table. Today I recalled nothing.

Helplessness, Martin says, is the most rewarding state of all.

———

I'd been reading about the brain because I'd been reading about Agnes Martin, and much of what I'd been reading about Agnes Martin claimed she was a paranoid schizophrenic.

An exceptionally high-functioning paranoid schizo-phrenic—psychiatrists consulted in the biography agreed upon that.

She couldn't have built five buildings. Or written so many essays and poems and parables. Or given so many talks.

She couldn't have been so regulated and regimented and self-reliant.

Couldn't have bicycled across the country or canoed Lake Powell.

She couldn't have planned her paintings; began her paint-ings; or finished her paintings. She couldn't have painted with such decisive rigor, such surety of vision, such acute aware-ness of feelings of pleasure.

Characterizing her as a paranoid schizophrenic bothered me. In that story, her choices are undercut by disease. Her hermitage, the concealment of her sexual orientation, even her strictness about the music she played (only Beethoven) could all be read as part of a grand coping strategy, denial on a massive scale, a way to avoid the conditions that trig-gered breakdowns and madness. (In the early seventies, when *Artforum* sent Lizzie Borden to the mesa to interview her, Martin used that word: *madness.* She said she'd been raped multiple times. She said, when that happens, you go into a fugue state.) In that narrative, she is reactive, responding to voices or visions, hallucinations. In that story, she retains so little agency.

Is that how she wanted to be seen?

I saw her as so powerful.

Situating yourself in a hammock when you're pregnant is an acrobatic maneuver. The book I was reading about the brain examined the relationship between creativity and neuropsychological disorders. I'd flipped to the index, to see if Martin was there; she was not. The prose was technical and dry. In the hammock, I'd started to get sleepy in the sun and skipped past the X-rays and MRIs of the brain to get to the art: Edvard Munch's *The Scream*, Louis Wain's hectic cats. Paintings and drawings created by people in mental hospitals. The work by schizophrenics was marked with bold lines, an accretion of wild imagery, compositions that bled off the edge of the page—the opposite of Martin's aesthetic.

Unlike Yayoi Kusama, who voluntarily committed herself to a mental hospital and spoke about the effects childhood trauma had had on her (she was painting early infinity nets in New York at the same time Martin lived in the enclave at Coenties Slip), pathology rarely entered Martin's self-presentation. Her essays include no mention of it; you'd have to be a biographist to read it into her writing. Her art—especially the paintings she made during the last thirty years of her life—radiates an anodyne serenity.

And this was the work I was drawn to. Back in the casita, I'd returned to plates of paintings from the eighties and nineties, images that made me feel rinsed clean and blank and still. *Untitled #2 1991*: a sheet torn from a pale-blue legal pad. *Untitled #7 1991*: six wide lanes of moth gray and five slender ribbons of a paler shade, hemmed in graphite. Pregnancy-test indicator colors, nursery colors.

Add to that her refusal to concede to a troubled mind. When an interviewer asked her about depression toward the end of her life, she said, "I have been happy every day." Asked in 1995 from "whom or what" she seeks inspiration, a question that seems subtexted, "Do you hear voices?" Martin replies, from "my mind." She was under the care of psychiatrists from the early sixties on yet she refused to let diagnosis steer the conversation from her art.

Perhaps her power affirmed itself through the reality of her illness. Still, I felt deeply shameful about my interest in her psychology—it was the most obvious reason for my fascination with her. I was not a paranoid schizophrenic. I was a semi-recovered anorexic and bulimic, with depression—dysthymia, not major depression, not manic depression—and what a therapist had suspected was generalized anxiety disorder. I had my first panic attack during a summer thunderstorm in a soft serve shop, with lots of hanging plants, a poster of Monte Carlo on the wall, and a *Ms. Pac-Man* machine with greasy controls: I was thirteen. But girls and women with eating disorders—often invisible eating disorders—have found me since June 1998, a month after I was diagnosed with anorexia. I trust the power of the hunch. I believe in affinities, the chill in your bones that says, we're the same. I get you. I felt lurid, adolescent, and dumb, thinking I wasn't sick enough to get her. Then I turned to another painting, murmured at its hushed beauty, and forgot to doubt myself.

Gratitude (2001): a rare field of pistachio green.

————

After taking my blood pressure, my temperature, and my pulse, the nurse told me to remove my underwear. She handed me a Pepto-pink paper blanket, folded in a long rectangle. I was wearing a dress: I could just roll that up.

It was the end of March. I was alone in the fifth-floor examining room. I had asked my husband to stay in the waiting area. It was only our second time in this suite of offices in this tower at Cedars-Sinai, and walking from the parking meter down Third Street, I recognized the dance studio and the empanada walk-up, the launderette and the nanoscopic Birkenstock shop, the weird Third Street businesses east of Robertson. I wished I were still outside. With my dress bunched below my bra and the paper blanket covering me from the navel down, I saw it all over again, the worst eruption I'd had since Santa Fe.

I had ordered a pair of maternity jeans online. For a while, shopping for pants, I'd gotten excited in that hollow way I did buying clothes. I would hope, quite simply, that what I wore could change me. I'd checked mostly Goop pregnancy guides, to consider whether Gwyneth Paltrow's favorite jumpsuit,

Breton-striped top, cardigans, cropped trousers, editor's picks for leaky-day thongs, and maternity bras would look good on me. That's how delusional I was.

The jeans arrived. They were a deep indigo wash, with false condom pockets on either side of the fly. Attached to the waistband was a tube of stretch fabric the milky brown of an old bandage.

I pulled them on. They fit in the hips and the legs. Then, the stretchy fabric went up, up, all the way over my bra.

I modeled them like this for my husband. We stood in the living room laughing. Neither of us really understood how large my body would become.

"Could you just cut that part off?" he asked.

Instead of returning the jeans by mail, I'd taken them to A Pea in the Pod in Beverly Hills. My husband drove with me—he often drove with me, he liked driving with me. I liked it, too, when I wasn't feeling worried about needing his company.

I'd left him at a cafe. Good luck, he'd said. I tried to smile. It felt sick and fake.

In the store, the blond salesclerk cinched a mannequin's rhododendron-red wrap dress and greeted me. The tattered mailing envelope with the jeans was in my tote bag. I unfolded the jeans at the register.

"People love those," she said, "when they're further along. You're so tiny. Go, try things on."

I flipped through the clothes. Whenever I lifted a hanger, the clerk found me. I didn't like her. I was not *tiny*. I felt teased, called out for my non-tininess. It was a veiled insult, dressed as a ploy to get me to buy stuff. Did this woman think I was a moron? Was this a directive in the employee training manual: *Compliment the rag. She's taking a giant mucus shit and tearing her vagina, getting stitches in her perineum any day now.*

Waiting for the doctor, I tried to smooth out the paper blanket. I should've caught myself, I thought, I should've been able to stop. In hindsight, the cognitive flip was clear: I was thinking things like, *Sure, put the fitting rooms in the back of the store so passersby aren't subjected to awful pregnant bodies of women like me.* The store was rack-crowded and mallish: pregnancy *wasn't* Chanel.

I combed the racks, feeling awful: I didn't want to waste time shopping for maternity clothes. It was already a waste of money. No lipstick could hide this pig.

In the back of the store, the track lights flickered. The fitting rooms were small, curtain in lieu of door. With twelve garments on the rod, I could barely lift an arm without bumping an elbow or a knee or my ass into that curtain. I was already fat—how magnificently fat would I be at the end of these nine months? And I'd grabbed so much beautiful expensive shit to garb my fatness: yoga pants and matching racerback tanks, bamboo bras, dresses, T-shirts, button-downs, rompers—everything with a secret: a button-down expanded with side panels of stretch ribbed material; a bandage-style cocktail dress with compression fabric sewn into the tummy; a snug-busted baby tee Frankensteined with a flowy tunic.

In leggings, my thighs bulged; cellulite dimpled the fabric. In the dress, my hips ledged over with morbid flesh. In the singlet, my stomach—it wasn't a bump yet, just a bloated splodge—suffocated. I was drenched with sweat, my crotch, under my arms, down my spine.

Also, I wasn't breathing.

I'd been in the store a very long time.

I pounded a bottle of water in the dressing room. I'd used this as a trick to get myself out of a panic attack before—to, as my therapist put it, halt the deregulation.

Now I had to pee. I left the dressing room, holding a sleeveless chambray romper. The word *maternity* was nowhere on the romper. No secrets, no stretch: a Humpty Dumpty silhouette, a playsuit for an overgrown child.

"That's it?" the clerk said. She sounded disappointed.

"Is there a bathroom?"

"Of course." She smiled sympathetically.

I was part of the club.

A stand steamer guarded the doorway between the final sale rack and the stockroom, where the bathroom was located. A dusty window let in tea-gray light. I peed, shut my eyes, and tried to stop the jittering in my brain. When I opened my eyes, it hurt to blink. I ran the hot water, and in the mirror above the sink, I saw my face coming apart.

"You're fine you're fine you're fine," I whispered.

By the time I handed the clerk my credit card, I was trembling. It wasn't an even exchange. I owed another twenty-eight for the romper. Two hundred dollars to clothe a body reduced to its basest female function.

I put on my sunglasses and walked toward the parking garage. Gorgeous women were leaving Intermix, sauntering into Sephora, alone, with friends, on phones, in perfect matching yoga sets, with chevron-quilted Gucci pochettes, schlepping shopping bags from Louis Vuitton like I schlepped my holey canvas bags from Ralph's.

I needed to get to the car. I would stand there and cry, a surge of big body-racking tears. I would sit on the ground in front of the car, against the wall. It was underground, it would be like being dead, no one would see me. When all this passed, I would text my husband.

Then I heard his voice.

"Hey, J!" He waved, holding a pair of cold drinks, a big smile on his face.

I cringed.

"I got you a decaf iced Americano," he said. "I was just coming to look for you. Did you find any nice stuff?"

I winced. Didn't he see? His hand hovered over my back, testing whether to touch me. I yanked away. I was shaking, squeezing back tears behind my sunglasses, barely breathing. I clenched my teeth.

"What kind of good stuff do you think a piece of shit like this can find?" My voice was under my breath, like a person talking to herself.

"What are you talking about?" he said. "JoAnna . . ."

We were moving, walking toward Santa Monica Boulevard. This was worse than Santa Fe. I was sober. I had no excuses. This was cloudless, warm, perfect Southern California. My husband was carrying my bag. He had to carry a useless pregnant person's things. Like carrying a sign that said MY WIFE IS A RECEPTACLE.

I said that to him. I spat the word *vessel*.

We got to our car in the garage, and it got worse. I got louder, I was crying so hard that I was gulping air, coughing when I tried to breathe. What was I saying? It was pointless, all of it, and I was tired of pretending there was a point. It made me sick, how inevitable it seemed . . . All this up and down, fear and hope, worrying about food and worrying about writing, when really, there was only one solution: I needed to kill myself. I needed to kill myself without hurting the baby. Was that possible? How premature was not too premature? Could I make it that long? In a sort of numb, caged way? If the baby could be taken out of me, I could be euthanized. Like a dog. Except I was less than a dog. I should be so lucky to be as good, as pure, as loving as Lucy. I was greedy, vain, superficial, and I would never be good enough—I hated how cliche and narcissistic this made me: another reason to kill myself now.

"Take the baby out of me and go live with your parents," I said to my husband. "They're good people. Or start looking for another woman now. I don't care. I'll help you. One of your students? Fuck her. I don't care. You should. You should. I'm sure plenty of your students would like to, one of those girls . . . who is pretty and happy and young, who's not a messed-up, garbage piece of shit. Because that's all I am . . ."

Etc. etc. etc. etc.

We sat in the parking garage for a long time. A woman climbed into her navy Escalade and backed out. A Volvo pulled in.

"You're none of those things, J." My husband's tone changed. "And I'm not going to start, as you put it, fucking another woman."

"You're wasting time." I was crying harder, because he didn't see this was the truth. "You're wasting money sitting here. You should let me go so I can . . . You don't deserve this. You could be so much happier without me, I know it, all right? Just accept it."

I couldn't remember what else he'd said, if he'd yelled or argued or been scared. I didn't know how long we'd sat there or how long I'd cried or how I finally came out of it. It made me want to die all over again, confronting how harmful I'd been. In the doctor's office, I replayed our silent drive home, east down Wilshire, past Farmers Market and The Grove, right on La Brea, left on San Vicente, past the new Sprouts, cresting the hill by weird, overstated Midtown Crossing, San Vicente becoming Venice, a hundred dough-nut shops, men on medians hawking feliz cumpleaños carna-tions, KFC where I'd once seen a guy in the drive-through change the next car up's tire, Virgil Video with the *Superstar* cutout, sidewalk grill outside Fallas at Western, CVS, Food 4 Less, or was it Smart & Final? Back to our neighborhood,

Hidalgo Car Wash, a sign painted on Manteca-white bricks across from the ARCO.

I heard voices through the walls, women in rooms around me. Laughing. The snick of a door. I was anxious for the doctor to come in. Out the window, I saw the hills, a slaughterous tinge of sunset.

I'd rehearsed the bullet points with my therapist. I would be calm. Factual. I'd read a lot of *Pregnancy 411*. I knew about baby blues. Hormonal spikes. Postpartum depression. Given my history—the suicide attempts, the resulting stint in a psych ward—it seemed responsible to ask a doctor if this was normal, prenatal ambivalence—normal, for a person like me.

I needed to tell the doctor so if I did . . . something to myself the onus wouldn't be on my husband.

Now I wished I hadn't made him stay in the waiting room. At my first appointment, he'd taken a photo of me mock-stricken beneath another paper blanket; pre-ultrasound, he'd captured me pliéing in a hospital gown. I could be irreverent with him. I could be composed and only a little hysterical as the phlebotomist drew my blood. I wouldn't be vulnerable with the doctor: I'd be calm. I wouldn't convey how terrifying it was, my brain dissolving.

There was a knock. Thigh-gap Jennifer had recommended getting to know all the doctors in the practice since any one of them could be doing the delivery. The doctor this afternoon was Dr. Tan, a man in a white coat in his forties or fifties. He wore a gray button-down. No tie. He had a shadowy mustache and a back-combed cloud of black hair.

He shook my hand. His hands were waxy, cold. He asked me what I did. I told him I was a writer and a professor. This seemed to please him. He nodded and adjusted the examining table until I was horizontal. Gingerly, he lifted the blanket and touched my belly. It was still strange to me, the firm lump of it: a tumorous muscle. He pressed my pelvis, nudged around my kidneys, and replaced the blanket.

"Looking good," he said, singsongy. He sat down at the computer and keyed notes. Then he spun toward me. His white coat was open, his fingers spread across his thighs. "Questions?"

I wanted an elective C-section, I told him. Even though it was a long way off, I wanted to be sure it was in my file. He looked upset. Why would I want *that*?

"It's the pain," I said, quietly. "I have friends who were in labor for twenty-four or thirty-six hours. I would rather . . . know what's going to happen, when."

These were my husband's friends' wives. I'd heard about their contractions, their tearing, their stitching, their post-delivery immobility. I didn't want those kinds of stories told about me, play-by-playing centimeters of dilation like football yards.

"That's not something all of us do," Dr. Tan said. "If there's not a medical imperative, it's considered . . . There's a lot more risk to the mother and the child. It's not advised. There's a reason that vaginal delivery is called natural childbirth. Because it's natural. A C-section is a major surgery. Every surgery comes with risks. Anything else?"

"My weight," I said. "Am I gaining too much weight . . . ?"

His eyes went to the screen; he scrolled, exasperatedly. The tiny mouse wheel zipped.

"No, your weight is completely on target. You shouldn't be worrying about gaining too much weight. This is not the time for that."

I nodded. "Okay," I said. "I just . . . okay."

"Anything else?" he said.

When I described to Dr. Tan how depressed I'd been, the table was reclined. "Confessing is a supine activity," writes John Berger. The paper blanket, which he'd moved aside to examine my belly, was repositioned across my lap. I looked down my body: if I focused, I could see a whorl of pubic hair through the pink.

I spoke as objectively as possible. "I have a history of eating disorders: anorexia, bulimia, EDNOS. I also have dysthymia and anxiety." I propped myself up on my elbows, how I would've done crunches last month. "Lately, I have experienced . . . a lot of suicidal ideation. Passive suicidal ideation. I haven't written a note. No plans . . . But. I have suicide attempts in my past, and this is . . . alarming."

"When were your suicide attempts?"

"Fifteen years ago," I replied.

"What kind of attempts?"

"Overdoses. Pills."

No reaction.

"It's frightening," I said, nervously. Maybe I'd been *too* objective. Too downplaying. "I think about how my body is serving this utilitarian purpose—carrying the baby—and it makes me feel so . . . disposable."

"Why would you feel disposable?" He sounded mildly vexed. "Why would carrying a child make you disposable? It is an incredible gift. A profound responsibility."

I leaned forward. His tongue poked behind his upper lip and bulged out the flesh.

"I think about how I should be happy right now, and I'm not. I've been so scared." It was an understatement. I kept trying. "Then I think the baby doesn't deserve that. So, when the baby is born, the baby will be better off without me. The baby shouldn't have a mother . . . thinking these things. Imagining her body in a dumpster. I shouldn't be feeling so . . . I don't know, dehumanized or invalidated by this. I just want to know how people deal with these feelings."

The examining room was cold. I caught a whiff of sterile gauze, old rubbing alcohol, like a phantom nurse readying my injection.

Dr. Tan looked at me with the expression of someone regarding an outré work of art. My husband got this way around Jeff Koons.

"What you're telling me is very, very troubling," he said. "This is serious. Do you understand? I should be calling up the orderlies and having you taken to the emergency room for a psychiatric evaluation."

"I'm not *going* to kill myself—I *think* about it. I think how it would be good to be gone."

"Let me be honest with you," he said. "This is not normal.

These are not feelings people 'handle.' This is in the top 10 percent of the worst things I've ever heard from a woman in your shoes. This is serious. It raises in me a good deal of alarm, as your physician. It's not just *your* anxiety or *your* anorexia, all right? You're a mother now. You have a new life inside you. A life to think about, which means thinking about a person other than yourself. It sounds to me like you've built your whole identity around being depressed, around your eating disorder, around thinking of yourself . . . this way . . . and I don't know how that served you in the past, but right now you're being selfish. You're endangering this new life. And now you need to think about what's best for this baby. This little baby inside you, the baby that *you're* carrying. You're caring for. This baby, you're its mother. All right? You're a mother now. You're here because you wanted this. If you're going to be a mother, you need to act like one."

I was silent.

He wheeled back to face the computer. "Are you seeing a psychologist?"

"Yes."

"And you've told that person about these thoughts?"

"I have."

"Have you ever been on antidepressants?"

"Yes. Celexa. In high school. For a year."

"Why aren't you taking anything now? Why hasn't your psychologist prescribed you anything for this?"

"I don't like medication," I said.

His brow furrowed. I could see then that behind his

indifferent expression, he was scowling. He turned toward me again and held up his left hand.

"If I get stung by a bee," he said, pointing to the meat of his palm. "If I get stung by a bee, and you know I'm allergic to a bee sting, what are you going to do?"

I blinked.

"You're going to stick me with an EpiPen. Or call 911. You're going to give me the drug that will neutralize the poison in my body. If I'm a diabetic, and I go into a diabetic coma, you're going to give me the insulin."

"Right," I said.

"Your brain is producing chemicals that are . . . I don't want to say poisoning you, but, in a sense, they are. They're poisoning you. They're making you think those thoughts are true. And they're not. Those thoughts aren't right. This is not what a woman in your position should be thinking. The medicine will counter that. That's what Zoloft will do."

"You can write the prescription. I won't take it," I said flatly.

"Why not?"

I sat up on the examining table. I tucked the blanket around my legs like a pencil skirt. "I'm not asking for medicine. I'm asking if there's anything *I* can do—exercise, changes to my diet, yoga, whatever."

"All of that is fine," the doctor said, "but if your system is trying to fight off poison, deep breathing isn't going to help. Think about your baby. Think about the mother you want to be for your baby. That's all you need to worry about right now. Being a good mother to that baby. I am strongly, strongly encouraging you to take the Zoloft."

The room buzzed with silence. "Right," I said.

He got up, pulled aside the curtain shielding the door, and left. I wadded up the blanket and shoved it into the garbage. The can was full. The crumpled paper stuck up over the lid.

I found my husband in the waiting room.

"How did it go?" he asked.

I shook my head.

In the car, I told him. What the doctor had said, what the doctor had prescribed. I was terrified my husband would be mad at me. As if my rages weren't enough, here was confirmation I was *truly* fucked up: I didn't want to follow medical advice.

"No. That's wrong," my husband said. I could see the color in his face: he was seething. "This is the problem with our healthcare system. With medication. Our country. This guy sees you, what, ten minutes? That entitles him to question your entire life and put you on an antidepressant? How does he know how you'll react to it? He's not a psychiatrist. He doesn't know you."

I felt oddly defensive. "He's probably trained to—"

"To what? Make rash judgments? To brush you off? What if you *weren't* happy to be a mother? What if you'd been assaulted, what if you'd been raped?" He punched the steering wheel. "Who the fuck does he think he is?"

"I'm not filling the prescription. Are you okay with that?"

"I would never take that. Never. But I'm not you."

"I'm hungry. Want to get an early dinner?"

We went to a French bistro hidden inside a strip mall. I ordered a coupe of champagne and took two sips. We sat, legs touching, at the bar. We ate caramelized endive and burgers and Paris–Brest. "I'm so angry," my husband kept saying. "I'm so angry." We got home and the moonlight fell, shell gray, on the bed. We fucked and he gathered my hair into a long ponytail and yanked it back.

That night, after my husband went to sleep, I sat in bed with my notebook. I wanted to write, and I couldn't. I stared at the ripples in the wall plaster. My attitude had shifted. Even if the shift were not permanent—of course it wouldn't be permanent—I could learn from this. The doctor couldn't help me. My therapist couldn't help me. Only I could help me.

A few weeks prior, bumming around on the internet, I'd read an article titled "Agnes Martin on How to Be an Artist." A photo of Martin as a stocky old woman in a canoe came up. Behind her, the sky was cumulus. The water was placid. Mountains. Fog. Smoke. She wore a parka. Her hair was Caesar short and mist white, her skin was lined, her mouth was set. I stared at her eyes, how directly they met mine, the irises jolting blue. The article swiftly dispensed with the schizophrenia-made-her-flee-New-York narrative and used her mental turmoil as a springboard into the hopefulness of her prose: "I believe in living above the line . . . Above the line is happiness and love . . . Below the line is all sadness and destruction and unhappiness. And I don't go down below the line for anything."

I wasn't yet sensitive to her contradictions. I didn't yet know she'd told interviewers she'd never been depressed; I didn't yet know in letters she'd written of "purest melancholy." I didn't yet know she'd used the word *madness*. I only knew what I felt in my gut—that if Martin had declared she didn't go below the line, there was a good chance she had been below that line and, surfacing, vowed not to go back.

I had to help myself.

I hated Dr. Tan's moralizing, and yet thinking about Agnes Martin, I knew, in a way, he was right. Having an eating disorder and depression and anxiety *was* integral to my self-concept. Perhaps, in being so open about mental illness, I'd kept my illness alive. I had prized sadness and destruction and unhappiness, nestled them against my heart like locks of baby hair in a dead locket, because for a long time, I had conceived of my own work in a state of purest melancholy. That wasn't right anymore. Martin's belief in happiness and love while living with schizophrenia made me want to do better. To change. After twenty years of therapy and treatment, I had *tools*; I was not using my *tools*. I was choosing to go below the line.

Above the line was reading, writing, and exercising—everything I'd been neglecting. If I wanted to change, I needed a plan. I drafted it in my notebook. I tried to make it manageable.

Write one poem a day.

Go to the gym, read on the treadmill.

In the morning, I would tell my therapist and my husband.

If a month of concentrating on this plan did not curb the suicidality, I would fill the prescription. I would take the Zoloft.
Putting this into words brought me great peace. I closed my
eyes. Lying in bed, I thought about Dr. Tan twisting on his
stool, screwing himself lower and lower. Soon he was a snake,
twisting on the ground, and I was high up on the examining
table, safe. Suddenly I could sit up.

7.

QUICK QUIZ:

Q. How long did Agnes Martin paint before she was pleased with a painting?

A. Twenty years.

Q. How long did it take her to paint a painting?

A. About three hours.

She might paint five hundred paintings in a year, keep ten.

Four hundred ninety paintings to the bonfire in a year! The interviewer from *Vogue* is aghast; Martin, characteristically unflappable. At eighty-five, she has been doing this half a century.

In bed, I smiled replaying the exchange. I'd come upon it that afternoon in my notes. Three days in, it was easy to stay out of my email and off the internet, to keep my phone in a suitcase, to not talk—sometimes, I didn't even speak to Lucy: she responded to a quick kiss-kiss.

Silencing the world, I was starting to feel like anything was possible. I loved coming to the end of the text box, rejigging a sentence or a paragraph so I wouldn't end mid-thought. I loved forcing myself to move on to the next box without reading over the words I'd just written.

Martin would approve of the efficiency, I thought. Somewhere, giving instructions to young artists, she talks about painting a canvas, turning it to the wall, painting nine more. Then seeing if anything was good.

I loved that kind of productivity, especially in the context of making art. It reminded me of The Factory (elsewhere, I'd read Martin liked Warhol, which tickled me) or how Russell Edson wrote prose poems, one after another, ripping the paper out of the typewriter, reloading, repeating, twenty in an hour.

I was good for three or four hours at the desk in the morning, another hour or two after lunch if I were lucky. No. Unswerving.

The problem was, I was itching to be out. I wanted to explore Martin's Taos. I wanted to find the art supply store where she bought her Liquitex acrylics, her one-inch red sable brush. I wanted to go to the Trading Post Café, where she ate lunch every day, holding forth at her table: I wanted to order a noon glass of chianti like she did, and whatever she liked for food. Did she have a regular order? Was she as routine at restaurants as she'd been on the mesa? I wanted to walk by the retirement community, spot nurses and staff smoking outside, ask about what it had been like in that small apartment where she spent the last twelve years of her life. I heard she hated it; I heard she loved it. "I don't have to think about anything but painting," she said of that time. I wanted to see the studio where she'd worked every day, eight thirty to eleven thirty.

That evening, my husband and I had gone to Martin's favorite bookstore. Or we tried to. By the time we drove into town, Brodsky Bookshop on Route 68 was closed. Inside, the owner was finishing up at the register; the store cat had settled in a black doctor's bag–style carrier. My husband pointed to a faded newspaper article about the screening of a new Martin documentary taped to the door.

"This is the bookstore she used to go to." Maybe the heat of the day, rising from the pavement, was getting to me: I sounded like a dozy tour guide. "It's been here a long time."

Martin insisted the store owner stock copies of the *Tao Te Ching*. She loved Agatha Christie novels. I told myself not to think about what I knew. Martin believed in "the Zen notion of intellect corrupting" perception, as Holland Cotter put it. I was trying to silence my intellect, embody the quiet state. Not telling my husband everything I knew was practice.

But it was hard. Especially with my stomach sticking out half a foot. Intellect was all I had. Beginning in preschool, my intelligence was applauded by all adults (save my parents). As a child, dull-looking and stout, I learned to rely on it, certainly to prize it above my physical appearance. Yet if I were going to see like Martin, if I were going to perceive, I needed to let go of that narrative. I needed to destroy it like one of those 490 paintings.

In bed, thinking about that interview, I wanted to hear her voice. There were two Martin documentaries but watching them would violate the internet rule. Only under true duress would I resort to that. Still, even if I couldn't hear her voice, I could imagine her tone: unboastful, unhampered—homespun, as one of my professors would say of certain poets, a term of highest praise.

The room was noisy. A dowel beat against the window-pane. I was lying on my side, facing my husband. He got hot at night. He had the ceiling fan going warp speed and a box fan oscillating at his feet. I couldn't sleep with air blowing over my body, blowing in my hair.

Several years later, my mother would tell me that when I was a toddler, she had to cut the tags out of all my clothes.

"A sensory thing?" I'd asked.

"You didn't like them touching you," she said.

Eventually, I'd cover my head with the rough brown sheets. But at the moment, I was just uncomfortable. My legs were heavy. I was aware of my bladder. My breasts were still growing—twenty-six weeks in, I was still touching them, surprised.

I rolled over to face the wall and remembered a good

friend's birthday was in a few days. Would I turn on my phone to text her? If I called her, would I hear about my friend's boyfriend? I thought of my friends, their different tastes in men, epitomized by the penis. While I had never described my husband's penis (even when it was my boyfriend's penis), my friends routinely described the penises of men they dated. One preferred a smooth penis, pubic hair trimmed, a silky shaft. Another wanted a thicket, head contusional, pronounced corona; she loved mapping the veins.

It was right, I thought sleepily, that the friend who preferred veininess had, for years, cut herself with safety pins and paper clips. The cuts were not so severe. Tallies, slashes, minus signs. I jolted in bed—the same grammar school orthography I saw in Agnes Martin's New York paintings when she felt, finally, she was on the right path.

I had cut myself like that, too. The cuts only occasionally bled. They red-lined a body, underlined channels where blood might flow and instead grew lethargic, frustrated, soporific, stopped up. A way to let the blood.

I inched to the edge of the bed, where I could no longer feel the heat beaming off my husband or the dog. *How has it been years since I cut myself?* I thought benignly. Perhaps these thoughts had been triggered by looking at *Flower in the Wind*. When Martin was nearly ninety, she named this painting from 1963 her favorite. The square canvas is covered edge to edge with putty-gray oil paint. A narrow border of this color frames the rectangle that consumes the rest of the canvas.

Tonight, if I prop the book up and walk to the other end

of the room, the rectangle resembles abraded skin. With the book on my bed—a different bed, without my husband or the dog—the rectangle comes alive: twenty-four rows of vertical lines. The rows are edged top and bottom by a firmer red that runs horizontal, like a smooth seam up the back of stockings. I try to imagine the four-inch reproduction exploded to its real-life seventy-five inches by seventy-five inches, three inches longer and wider than her standard six-foot canvas, how much power would radiate off the picture plane if one were to confront it on a wall.

Or no. Up close, I might confront the precarity of those vertical lines. The painstaking labor of lining up thousands of red toothpicks perfectly equidistant, touching/not touching close. Then doing it twenty-three more times. Then resolving to do it or starve.

It dawns on me: she had not always made three-hour paintings.

8.

My husband was shirtless, eating popcorn. He looked like a rugged fantasy of health, calves dripping sweat and grit after a run, sunglasses. Especially the sunglasses. He said, "I'm glad to be moving into a less hedonistic way of living with you."

"How have we been hedonists?"

Instantly I regretted it—it came out coyer than I meant it to. I didn't have time to be distracted with sex.

I was spitting cherry pits into a ramekin at the kitchen counter. I'd spent the morning at the desk, forehead inches from a book, reading and staring at things like Gianfranco Gorgoni's 1974 black-and-white photo of Martin on the edge of the mesa, with all of New Mexico valleyed below, and a plate of Martin's 1963 *Night Sea*, a lustrous field of peacock blue overlaid with a mesh-fine grid. Eleven years separated the woman in the photo from the woman who'd signed the verso or penciled up the stretchers of the painting, but both women exuded a kind of understated majesty—one surveying nature in all its vastness, the other forging a nearly six-foot grid out of gold leaf. The effort was staggering to me. Back in grad school, I'd worked for a pastry chef in Chicago, and sometimes, plating desserts, I'd garnish with gold leaf. Food-grade gold leaf was impossible to handle—it came in a special hermetic plastic bag between sheets of parchment, and you needed tweezers or a pointy-tipped offset spatula to peel it up, and when you did it wilted and clumped at the slightest kitchen draft. It was unfathomable to me that Martin could've made such delicate, mechanically precise interstices with that material.

My husband braced himself against the kitchen counter and stretched his back. He had a few freckles on his trapezii. I could smell the dusty road on him, the big sun.

"How have we been hedonists?" I asked again, reluctantly.

"Anytime we prioritize easy indulgence over effortful pleasure," he said. "When the extra effort is actually satisfying. Ordering food instead of preparing a meal."

My husband often celebrated us. He'd observe something we did—say, honeymooning in France for three weeks out of one carry-on—with a mythmaker's eye. I wondered if he'd do that with the baby, too—if he'd be the kind of father who made you feel special and loved. He presented his compliments in a sincere, serious way, after a pause elegant as a caésura.

It had happened a few days earlier, driving north on 87, around aureate Dalhart, Texas (home of the Golden Wolves, Sun Brite Laundromat, Hodie's Bar-B-Q's gold-lit arrow, Hotel Rita Blanca). We'd been moving in and out of talking, in and out of silence. Red and blue lights pinwheeled in the wind, a police car parked outside a home for at-risk youth and mothers—a place not unlike the shelter in Taos, to which Martin once out-of-the-blue wrote a check for $75,000. In Dalhart, we started seeing billboards for New Mexico. Right after Happy State Bank and Toot'n Totum, an ad for a town called Raton: *Your pass to the good life exploreraton.com.*

In the hammock I'd learned that Jack Kerouac was schizophrenic; on the internet, I'll learn he mentions Raton (emphasis on *tone*, Spanish for *mouse*) in *On the Road*.

"'Last chance to sleep in Texas,'" my husband read.

"Forget Taos," I said. "Texline Inn's $49.99."

We drove out of the last expanses of western Texas. Soon we were on the Santa Fe Trail. I thought, *Poetry is a form of landscape.* I saw a sign: WELCOME TO CIMARRON, WHERE THE ROCKIES MEET THE PLAINS! The mountains loomed in the distance, the chiaroscuroed blue of high clouds.

"I don't know anyone else doing this," my husband said.

"Neither do I."

At that moment, I liked being exceptional. Sometimes,

I could let the comment land and feel content; other times, when I was irritated with myself, the kindness only enflamed my disappointment with myself, and I was a contrarian.

In the casita, I rubbed my throat. I pushed away the cherry pits. I agreed with him, but the sentiment still annoyed me. Tell me I'm not indulgent, I'll lap cream.

My husband began eating popcorn in the overblown way (unanorexic) people do, tossing handfuls into his mouth. The more I watched him, the angrier I got at myself for taking a lunch break. This was probably the first thing my husband had eaten today. He'd also decided to stop drinking. He'd also been going on two-hour runs. He'd also been experimenting with fasting. And he'd never needed breakfast to begin with. I tried not to linger over all this—it was hot how he made abstinence look like hedonism.

"Have I told you I love this place?" he said.

"New Mexico?" Later, in Mary Lance's documentary, I'd see an eighty-something Martin wearing a cornflower-blue sweatshirt, appliquéd with the words NEW MEXICO. Being here made you want to record being here.

"And a house like this. The temperature, the light."

My husband was effortless in his noticing. He had a meditation practice. He was methodical and thoughtful, whether he was chopping an onion or writing a stanza. I was frenetic, compulsive, anxious without my notebook or the Notes app on my phone. I undid the whole kitchen; I wrote in a tear. And it was the hectic rushing quality that made me feel so ashamed and misguided when I read Martin: "You cannot run and be very aware of your inspirations." Only, I wasn't allowed to run.

"I do, too," I said. I really did. It was simple and beautiful. Good light and a good temperature because the adobe kept the inside cool during the day, and at night the temperature dropped, and we could let a breeze come in the screen door. Even the dry heat or the cool air made me think about Martin. She'd chosen this climate.

Or, she'd come to New Mexico because it was cheap, as she said in one interview. The poorest state in the union.

I got up. I threw out the pits. I kissed my fingertips, pressed the kiss to my husband's slick back, and wiped the sweat on my shirt.

"Back to work?" he said. He sounded disappointed.

"Back to work."

———

I had to get back to work because the morning was shit. I couldn't remember if I'd finished a text box. The only writing I'd produced were debt calculations in my reading notes.

5900-1500=4400
+ 250=4650
BP=4100+TD 2100
BP=1800,
TD(2)=-1700,
100/debt gone 08-01 latest

And on and on. Numbers filled the header, where one might put the date. I hadn't recorded the date. The penciled takeaways of my reading—quotes and bullet points, whole paragraphs of Agnes Martin's writing and Nancy Princenthal's biography; Nancy Andreasean's study of writers and mental illness; Eric Kandel's research on neurological disorders and creativity—were distracted by the raving arithmetic of someone with an overtaxed Visa.

I'd been up at four thirty, not talking, writing. I was keeping my desk in the spare room neat. When I walked in, it looked like the desk of someone who respected their work. A laptop and a notebook. I paid special heed to Martin when she veered prescriptive. I loved concrete directives. If she told me to try writing with a charred stick, I would.

"You clean and arrange your studio in a way that will forward a quiet state of mind," she says. "This cautious care of atmosphere is really needed to show respect for the work."

But this morning, I was too stressed about money to write very long. I'd closed my laptop and opened my notebook, where the numbers had poured out of me in relief.

Numbers were integral to Martin's process. The flyleaf in one of the books was a zoomed-in version of the math behind her paintings. When she saw that postage-stamp-size image of the painting in her mind, she'd have to work out the proportions for her six-foot (later five-foot) square canvas. (I didn't, and don't, know if her prints or works on paper—typically one-sixth or one-fifth of the size of her works on canvas—warranted the same calculations.) Behind every painting were sheets of paper covered with multiplication and equal signs, pluses, the jaunty checkmark of long division. A sprawling cursive math. It's not easy, a lot goes into these, balancing the lines, she says in the documentary where she wears the New Mexico sweatshirt. The camera lingers on her blue ballpoint numerals—it loves them like I do. Very *A Beautiful Mind*, *Good Will Hunting*.

Those pages where she showed her work: chaotic emblems of process. Her numbers were evidence of her art; my numbers, everything that distracted me from my art.

The income was teaching or freelancing or gig work, the deficit was who knows how many hedonistic choices—a $700 F97 Chanel blazer in pumpkin and russet tweed with gorgeous tortoise buttons from a vintage shop on Melrose, $7 oat mochas from Blue Bottle, $200 facials on Robertson, another $48 order of Night+Market Thai. The baby should not have a mother with consumerist impulses, especially if the baby's mother is a writer, especially if the baby's mother is in debt.

I was doubly pathetic. I was ashamed of debt and ashamed that I'd let this base fuckup infect my studio, my unwritten page.

Because only a few weeks before we left, one night in June, an hour after I'd fallen asleep, I awoke jerked by what could've been inspiration, when I could've scrawled in my notebook or jotted a note in the Notes app; when I could've remembered an idea that resonated from my reading; when I could've run down to my office, footfalls clomping on the creaky stairs (in another year, see me stage-tiptoeing to keep from waking my son); I could've torn through reproductions of Agnes Martin's paintings, searching the books for a painting, any painting; when I could've let myself be moved by *Milk River*, erasing midnight, aiming a light on the image, breathing the quiet sulfur smell of the new pages, looking from the mottled paint of the tawny border to the wash of cream to the red lines drawn slender with colored pencil, imperfect, crepitant, sod-red lines that Agnes Martin had slit into oil paint, guided by a taut string; instead I'd logged into the banking app.

It was a night I got paid. The balance in my checking account meant I could schedule a credit card payment.

When I anticipated a direct deposit, I slept lightly. When the credit card debt (my husband named it *consumer debt*, with great tact) had been worse, I'd wake up at 2:00 a.m. so I could see money appear in my checking account. Then the relief of subtraction: my balance, newly grown, would diminish as I transferred cash to one or (usually) several credit cards.

For a time, I'd eliminated the debt. I thought this would end my account monitoring: It didn't. I'd get anxious, absent, hungry in the mouth and indifferent to food. I'd log in, pause, look at the money, and transfer it to a high-interest savings account; a dull, fugacious numbness would come over me. "Never seek sustenance through human schemes," writes Teresa of Ávila, "for you will die of hunger—and rightly so."

Material hunger, I was convinced, had killed me.

How little do you need? I wrote over and over in my notebook before we left.

At my desk, I opened my laptop. The internet was off, the time was hidden, the cursor was still blinking in a text box.

Martin had lived poor, I knew. Between stints at Columbia, when she was offered the teaching position at University of New Mexico, she "built a house and went in debt." Until Betty Parsons paid for her to relocate to New York, there wasn't a time she wasn't working—her last year of grad school, three jobs. The way I looked at it, her poverty—especially on the mesa—was chosen and noble.

————

Credit Alois Riegl, the imperial-mustached founder of the Vienna School, with coining the term neuropsychologist's still use to the describe the creative mental process undergone by viewers of art: *beholders share*. Command and possession, staring and ingesting, the obvious eroticism in the word *behold*. From the Old English *bihaldan*: bi, *thoroughly*, haldan, *to hold*.

As in, I was thoroughly held by *Untitled #7*.

So held I forgot my meager holdings.

The *Untitled #7* I beheld that afternoon was from 1991. The reproductions were misleading about the size of the canvas. *Untitled #7* was still six feet by six feet, the size Martin painted on for another three years. With *Untitled #8* she scaled down to 60 1/4 inches by 60 1/4 inches. A year later, the quarter inch fell away, and she'd paint the remainder of her life on five-feet-by-five-feet squares.

Two coats of gesso—more would strip the tooth from the

canvas. A strap-like measuring tape guides her graphite lines. Then, she applies acrylic paint, thinned to a wash with water, leaving faint brushstrokes on the surface

This was a three-hour painting: wide bands separated by narrow belts of pale pink, stitched off by the graphite defining the lines, bounding the acrylic. The acrylic: fleshy bivalve pink that pools in the corners and lightens as the eye moves up. By the time you reach the top left quadrant, the color is bleachy and vacant, a half-thought.

As I looked at the painting, the color seemed to split: half in shadow, half lit—as lit, anyhow, as the murky pink of a brain suspended in formaldehyde. As I looked, thinking about *Untitled #7* with its wide lanes and *Night Sea* with its pointillistic gold leaf, I couldn't help thinking you could sell more three-hour paintings than the alternative.

I closed the book and held it in my lap. Beheld it against my belly. Because *Untitled #7* was reproduced in this book, I was holding *Untitled #7* and *Untitled #7* was also holding me holding the baby, all without the painting witnessing the exchange.

9.

I MADE ONE TENTATIVE LOOP around the first floor of the Harwood—I felt like a stalker doing a drive-by. I was not prepared for the early paintings hanging on the walls right outside the Agnes Martin Gallery. I was not prepared to be around other people, casually looking at the work. I saw the Martin Gallery and immediately spun around. I found the bathroom and retreated to the last stall, where I took out a notebook and wrote, shaking:

> After a morning reading Glimcher's reflections and AM's writing, lectures, after looking at every painting, after

half a sack of cherries, after a morning at my desk,
just reading and looking until my thoughts stop
and it feels like listening, here, seeing AM's Nude,
from 1947, with straight short blunt bangs and
heavy breasts in that wide gold frame with the
green-blue globbed thick, just glimpsing the AM
Gallery through the doorway, tears, stunned now
I'm shaking in the bathroom and some machine is
humming and I am grateful for these weeks, when
did I last fall so fully into another life? It is like
being in love or finding a mother.

———

At first, I was alone in the gallery. It was smaller than I'd ex-
pected and yet it didn't feel small. Lightness came from two
sources: the oculus overhead, which let in the sky, and the
paintings themselves, their incredible luminosity.

The entryway to the gallery was wide. Certainly the people who'd first conceived of this space, who loved Martin's
work, understood this suite of paintings would require a dis-
tant viewpoint to take in the work as a unit. There were the
seven paintings, *Untitled* with parenthetical subtitles.

I stood on the threshold to the space and caught myself
doing something I rarely did: I touched my belly.

All seven paintings contained common traits: the horizontal line and the colors—custardy yellow, blue like a mist
over the ocean. Unlike *Milk River* or *Night Sea*, there was no
sense of a ground pigment on these canvases, no frame within

the frame. The frames were silver metal. The horizontal lines stretched right to the edge.

I started on the left and went clockwise around the paintings. Being in front of them, I noticed the nearly imperceptible intensities of color, a point of pressure in the graphite. But those details refused to stay in focus. Looking at one after another in this space was like looking at clouds on a hot day when you haven't eaten, when you're lying on a blanket next to your lover who's fallen asleep, when you're so in love it seems impossible the world can encompass so much beauty; you look at a smear of cloud, the sun blinds you, you close your eyes, the cloud has shifted, the cloud is a new cloud, the cloud is three clouds or seven clouds, you close your eyes, you open them, you sink into the woozy joy, recognizing the same sky.

I went from canvas to canvas. I counted eight equal bands in one; three wide bands and four narrow bands in another. Then I stopped. I sat down on one of the yellow cube benches beneath the oculus.

I had a notebook in my tote bag. I picked it up and put it down.

I didn't want to put my response into numbers or words. I wanted to hold it in my body, the force of this beauty. And perhaps the beauty had even taken hold of my body because the baby began kicking. He was squirming on the right, below my ribs, rhythmically kicking. I could see his heel bouncing the front of my dress. It was a wrinkled linen thing, with short sleeves and scooped neck, creamy buttons down the front, pumpkin orange, and the kicks pressed the fabric outward. My little reproduction reproducing the immaterial quality of my emotional response to the work. If the women in the gallery were to turn from the paintings, they would've seen the baby's foot.

The women in the gallery didn't turn. They were here for Agnes Martin, they told a security guard. He'd gone over to them; now they were talking.

"Friends recommended this. Highly," said one woman.

The guard was nodding. "Did you know Agnes Martin's last request was to be buried under a tree behind the museum?"

Apricot tree, I added silently. Sometimes, when people were talking, between pauses, I played a game with myself to see if I could complete the sentence or guess the next word. Recently, doing this with my husband, I'd supplied the phrase *pomp and circumstance*. I did not interrupt or blurt the word—not often, really—and yet the game made me feel stupid and smug, going around spoiling all the little surprise parties of life.

The women smiled broadly. "Good for her!"

In my mind, I told everyone to leave. My legs crossed prissily high: I spread them. The tote bag at my feet vanished. The front of my dress flattened. The sky dusked. The Rio sluiced the gallery. The writing in my notebook ran. The Rio splashed early nudes, juvenilia in the archives, everything Martin had renounced. Water at my ankles, at my knees, coming into me, sloshing the baby, clutching my neck, rising above the paintings, loosening them from their mounts

(the detail about Martin liking that she'd been born the year
the *Titanic* sunk).

All at once I was alone. The women had left. The guard's
voice was in the hall.

I held my stomach and covered the baby. The Agnes
Martin Gallery had been designed to hold the paintings permanently and to invite interference from the sky. To put it
plainly, the oculus let in different qualities of light and the
different qualities of light influenced the paintings. I looked
up: the sun was shining too bright to see through the dirty
glass.

———

It was eighty-eight degrees when I left the Harwood, and the
heat still lingered at dinner. I tossed pea shoots with good
olive oil and lemon and the cured black olives I love, shriv-
eled and treacly as dates. I rumpled slices of prosciutto and
nestled a little burrata on each of the salads.

"What's wrong, J?" my husband asked.

"Nothing."

"Something's wrong."

"No."

"Will you tell me?"

I didn't understand my response to the paintings. I had
been moved, and then that feeling of having been moved
receded. The beauty was fading. I felt dumb. How could I
trust my own perception, my own sensibility, when it was the
viewpoint of two people rather than one? The baby's kicking

in the gallery haunted me. I reflected on myself—eyes pellu-
cid, mouth set firm so as not to quiver, staring luridly at her
moving belly, as though spotting a tick, a live brown period
sunk under the skin.

But why couldn't I look at the paintings with the baby?
Why couldn't that be nice? Why couldn't I accept that there
was no perfect, pristine, blank-slate consciousness from which
to view Martin's art? When so easily I could recall what she
told Jill Johnston: "It's forever raining when the sun is shining."

Eventually, I tined the curlicue of a pea shoot. "I'm having
a . . . mean thought."

"Okay, good," my husband said. He took another piece of
bread. "This tastes perfect."

I shook my head, angry. He knew my sullen pattern, and
he was ignoring it.

The thought cinched around me like a belt. It had been
building all day, since that morning, reading Glimcher and
learning more about Agnes Martin's studios—even when I'd
initially believed I was calming down, the thought was there.
Driving back from the museum, into the washed pastel of
mountains, the thought was surging, with the disassembled
crib in the back of the car.

I did not want to leave. I did not want to leave with my
husband. I wanted to stay here alone.

I would never be anything if I could not find solitude.
I would be a failure and unhappy with myself forever and
unhappy with other people. I had almost stepped inside Martin's space on the mesa, I could see it, that crude hangar of

a building, vigas and latillas and linoleum. A fluorescent-lit storefront in a strip mall, where she kept a cot (no pillow) and two chairs: a folding chair for viewing the paintings, a rocking chair for herself. Geraniums. And the studio she rented in downtown Taos she left unlocked because what was there to steal? Only paintings. I had copied out and starred in my notes: "The artist of course is a natural person but it is necessary for him to stand against societies' conventions and against his natural inclinations in order to do his work."

Lucy's tail swished on the brick floor. She was waiting for cheese, and burrata was a mess to share. Across the room, *The Silence of the Lambs* sat on the coffee table. We had started reading it aloud at night. On the cover, a graceful hand, a pianist's hand or a realistic dummy's, cupped a moth with persimmon-colored wings.

"What do you want me to say?" my husband asked. "I have 'mean thoughts' all the time. Do you want me to share them?"

Yes, I screamed in my head. I didn't want to have to get into it. I hated eating dinner together. I hated the grocery store. I hated how pleased I'd been with the idea for this dinner. I hated the simple, shareable pleasure of food. There had been a preview of this rage that morning, with the bunk bed and the game locker and the eiderdown chest, with the dull damp hump of the washing machine: I wished I had the nerve to open the side door and walk into the cold morning, to leave forever. Instead, I had told myself, *Shut up, shut up shut up shut up.* I narrowed my eyes on my husband. *Hurt me!* I thought.

Hurt me and give me a reason to feel hate and rage, a reason to annihilate myself, a reason to detonate this night, this marriage, this life. How else would I get away from myself?

"I don't know," I said. "Do what you want."

I pinched off a piece of cheese. The cream center oozed on my fingers. I gave the firm part to Lucy. Then a sudden tightness jolted my stomach.

"Are you okay, J?" he said.

"I'm fine."

It was such a lie, I almost winced. I listened to myself barely breathing. The baby had a 90 percent chance of surviving preterm. If he was done with me now, I would understand. We'd be forced to stay. Instead of alphabet quilts, I'd wrap our son in a river, a canyon, a gorge.

10.

Keeping a soft attitude is unavoidable when the heat conspires with the altitude. It melts your brain. By the end of the morning, it was ninety degrees and climbing.

I was after the soft attitude because Martin urged it. A soft attitude, Martin says, allows you to accept more. All morning I'd kept that soft attitude, and the work had been good. I wrote three hours before I decided to go for a walk.

Was it exercise or a reset? Reset. No. Reset sounded hard—hard reset was a sort of computer hack. This was a walk.

As soon as I stepped outside, the

heat settled on me. Below my feet, the gravel crunched. I walked slow, keeping my eyes on the scrub bordering the casita, where my husband had seen field mice and snakes.

But once I stepped out onto the dusty road, I started moving faster. I had always been a fast walker. Being pregnant wasn't going to compromise my pace.

Driving around, I'd seen neighborhoods, blocks of ranch houses and patches of grass, the ponderosa pines that filled the forests. But here, the desert was so vast and the mountains so close that the houses—already far apart—seemed as if they'd been dropped down at random, in a Surrealist game of chance. When I looked ahead, I could see the call box at the end of a long drive, a solid gate hung with Tibetan prayer flags: La Casa de Lopez, El Rancho de Bella Vida, the casita was surrounded: million dollars million dollars.

In the air, there was a rattle and an electric sizzle as though beneath the desert there were live wires. The sounds intensified in the heat.

I asked myself: Could I do this forever? Do I need more?

Moving through the torrid heat, I felt like I was breaking the invisible skin between dimensions. Now, if I were to see one of Martin's canvases, surely I'd be able to push through. Moving through the torrid heat, I felt no unfolding time—there was no time. There was a black butterfly wide as a Chinese star. Two white mariposas helixing over big sage.

I would only know "big sage" later. I was in the midst of a seventeen-day boycott of looking up—well, anything, including plant names. Facts were to be avoided, Martin said.

Facts filled the mind and a crowded mind could not welcome inspiration.

It was getting hotter. I peered down and sideways, into a culvert or a ditch-like trench, staring at plants and bones. When I tried to look forward and settle on one view, I felt dizzy. The desert laid out like burlap. I hadn't brought my phone, and it was surely after noon. No. I should not think about the time.

But I was not walking straight. I kept drifting to the center of the road, putting myself back on the shoulder, where the gravel is sand and litter:

99 Proof: 99 Black Cherry, 99 Green Apple, 99 Grape.

Small Fireball plastered to the grass.

Brown beer bottle glass broken prettier than stones.

There was nothing exceptional about being alone, I thought, shaking away the spots in my vision. I was not the only one who wanted it.

(Martin says: "I'm very careful not to have ideas because they're inaccurate.")

And I was not alone. One Texas Lexus, two Texas Lexus. Black and black.

I kept looking for a white Mercedes. A white Mercedes E320, like the one Martin drove at ninety. Martin could fix your car. She'd had six of them on Portales mesa when Jill Johnston came to visit.

Outside an adobe office building with a sign that said CIELO AZUL, I thought: Could I do better than this? Could I give up more?

Yes yes yes, went a prairie dog in oboe tones, popping out from a hole in the front yard of Holy Cross Hospital.

I stopped for a moment. I had never seen a prairie dog. They looked like squirrels, but longer, tubier, and watching them the whole scene seemed to pause.

All at once, I was hot. Hot and so queasy. So queasy my vision was spinning, and my nose stung like the first chlorine seconds underwater. I didn't know where I was in relation to the casita. I had made a confused, amoebic circle.

I bent over and hung my head and shut my eyes. I was seeing spots. The spots were shifting, sputtering, moving around like a dark kaleidoscope. I'd just learned the word for this in Arkansas: *phosphene*.

I gripped my knees. I spat. The street signs for El Paseo Canon East, La Luz Road, were blocks back.

Slowly, I straightened up. I took in the antemeridian sky. Big, up-there blank page.

You're pregnant, I thought. *You're being stupid.*

Gradually, the road stopped disappearing. The light-and-a-half of reality returned. On the ground, amid the dust and rocks and roots and the dendritic tangles of dead plant matter and thistles, I saw a second small Fireball. Then a penny steps from a stop sign. I picked it up: both sides tails. The letters of *E Pluribus Unum* shook free. The heraldic crest scrunched into a heart. The coin was burning from the sun. It had a pulse.

———

That night, after dinner, my husband looked on his phone for a park to walk Lucy. She hated the gravel and refused to walk on the dirt roads around the casita.

We drove past secondhand shops and rodeo grounds aglow with cold spotlights on tall metal poles, and a garage spray-painted 4 RENT JOSE with a phone number in congealed red. We drove past a graveyard of scallop-edged headstones and dollish bouquets. Then we turned right into Fred Baca Park.

It was a nice municipal park with faintly sketchy vibes. Something about the empty tennis courts or the covered pavilion with picnic tables, the bottles and tallboy cans in the trash smacked of juvenile debauchery. Even juvenile debauchery—a subject near and dear to my writing heart— was not safe from the new fear I harbored. I caught myself worrying about our unborn son getting into drugs, like a parody of a parent in a nineties sitcom, and focused on the park.

Lucy sniffed and pulled. There was a football field encircled by a paved loop, and she trotted happily, with her weird bowlegged gait that made her look like a duck. She sniffed barbecue grills and prairie dog burrows; there were faint yips and chirps.

Beyond the park, there was a system of paths and trails, a subplot of preserved wetlands.

We crossed a footbridge. From the footbridge, we looked out at the marsh and saw a bird the size of a sizable piggy bank, plumper than an egret, gentler than a Cooper's hawk, bobbing, treading, upright, afloat. The bird sat in a reflection of the clouds on the water; it was part of the mirroring of the cattails and sedge, too.

Lucy tugged. My husband kept going. I caught up with them at a sign explaining the difference between a swamp and a marsh. The illustration was faded, and the text was worn off in places, as if by a fist of eraser. I could read only phrases and words. *Cienaga.*

It struck me that perhaps I needed Agnes Martin right now, in these months, because the awareness in my mind was changing. "Beauty is awareness in the mind," she writes. "We respond to beauty with emotion." I liked how Martin gave emotion a job—perhaps the best job.

Emotion was the spray of vowels in *cienaga*, a word that means swamp. I hadn't known that. It was the street I'd turned off, the last five months of prenatal appointments, a sweep from Beverly Hills to Hollywood, strip malls furniture showrooms restaurants bodegas boutiques, a rooftop bar on the corner of Melrose that tinted the Hills cichlid pink.

"The name makes sense," my husband said, reading beside me. "The tar pits, the oil fields."

The sky was darkening around us. The park was closing. It was time to leave. Emotion had nothing to do with feelings. It was the collision of stimulus and behavior, the pond, the marsh, sky pried from above and painted in the water, mosquitos starting to bug, Lucy and her sporadic courage on the bridge's shaky planks. What distinguished a marsh from a swamp, I learned, was the absence of trees. Herbaceous plants comprise a marsh. They would die and be reborn, sustained by the rich soil, waterlogged, braided with roots.

We walked toward the parking lot, past the playground. A family of two, a mother and her toddler, was getting in a few last swings.

"Do you love me so much?" the little boy called. His voice was light and beautiful.

"I love you so much," the woman called, pushing him. Her voice was beautiful, too.

"Do you love me so much?"

"I love you so much!"

The mounds of dirt punctured with tunnels. The creaky chains of the swing. I looked down and let my hair fall in my face. I was starting to cry.

11.

On the metered side of Civic Plaza Drive, a NO PARKING ANY TIME sign had been altered with two strips of white duct tape. The longer strip covered the word *parking*; the shorter strip covered the word *any*. The new sign read:

NO

TIME

My husband and I had noticed it our first night, during our slow tour of town. Now it was late morning. As we pulled into a spot across the street, I was pleased to see it again. A shiver of anarchic, fuck-the-man, death-to-capitalism glee ran through me: time is fiction, time is antimatter, time's a construct.

Only today the duct tape struck me as less punk than Zen. Zen erasure duct tape.

I'd inherited a copy of Shunryū Suzuki's *Zen Mind, Beginner's Mind* from a professor. A few days ago, after hours reading in the hammock, I'd come to the end of a section and splayed the book over my stomach. This was satisfaction. There had been light rain, there was a warm breeze. Sheer clouds hung over the sky, veiling the creeping orange sun. My body was awake and at ease; my mind was full and still. I was doing it: wandering into diligence.

I'd brought the book because it was tangential to Martin. Martin's relationship to Zen Buddhism—her interest in East Asian literature and philosophy, her proximity to D. T. Suzuki's Columbia lectures—was well documented in biography, and *Zen Mind, Beginner's Mind*, with Suzuki's brief essay chapters and soothing instructional tone, his faculty with abstract nouns like *time* and *contentment*, made an object lesson of its influence on her prose.

Sometimes I had to remind myself that Martin wasn't a strict Buddhist—the only strict anything she was was herself. According to art historian Suzanne Hudson, "Martin's pantheism became a seeking pluralism, sourced from Buddhism, Taoism, and Christianity . . . encapsulated by none of them . . . put simply, a do-it-yourself faith."

We got out of the car and set off for the galleries. I glanced back at the sign as we walked toward Paseo Del Pueblo Norte. I felt a twinge of wistfulness. I was excited to help my son develop the capacity to receive inspiration, to recognize beauty everywhere, to find it even in defacement. Yes. A do-it-yourself sensibility.

———

In June, we'd visited our married friends' townhouse in Evanston. Stacking rings, Sophie the giraffe, blocks on the rug, plugged-up sockets. The lady of the house danced (all right—moved her neck) in her high chair, a curly-haired, quinoa-puff-smashing ten-month-old. We were two thirty-something couples listening to George Michael, snacking on cheese that had been out so long the runny Époisses stank, playing a game called Concept.

"What part of having a baby are you most excited about, J?" my friend asked.

In Concept, you select a word or phrase from a card. Your task is to get the other players to guess that word or phrase, and to do so you communicate silently, through icons. You place translucent tokens on a board gridded with colorful icons. Translucent exclamation mark tokens go on concepts (Film, Food/Beverage, Man) and translucent cube tokens go on sub-concepts (Comedy, Blue, Sports). In this way, you get someone to blurt, "Waterboy."

I pinched a sticky apricot and dragged it through a smear of Brie. ("Do you do the whole unpasteurized thing?" my friend had asked. "Please *let* it be unpasteurized," I'd said.) I reconsidered her question as George Michael wailed—he was never gonna dance again.

"How he'll change me," I said finally. "How the baby will change my life."

Where had that come from? Blame the plaintive sax. Or the game: something dislodged from the subconscious by my guessing strategy, a blitzkrieg of free association in the name of obtaining a cardboard light bulb.

Ninety percent of my time in therapy the last year had been spent on concepts such as:

Fear of having child.

Fear of becoming mother.

Fear of becoming my mother at her worst: manipulative, unhappy, cruel, lost.

It was hard enough being a human being, harder being a woman human being, harder still being a woman human being becoming a mother, hardest of all becoming a mother when you're a woman human being whose reproductive urges have been satisfied by her art.

The obsession with Agnes Martin took that consternated, anxious fear and funneled it into productive, not-totally-solipsistic work. I'd nodded hard, reading critic Lucy Lippard's *From the Center*: "The concept of a female sensibility is our greatest burden as artists." I'd nearly fist-pumped when Martin flat-out asked *The New Yorker*'s Benita Eisler if she could tell whether her paintings were done by a man or a woman. My students would call Martin on feminism "problematic." I adored her for it: "The women's movement failed. They aren't any more free than they ever were." *They*?

And yet how much of my suspicion toward women, my animosity toward motherhood, was the result of a deep generational misogyny. Several years earlier, I'd frequented a community center with my grandmother to play bingo. She was ninety-seven. She wore a stained Chicago Bears fleece, polyester pants, and Velcro diabetic shoes. If a clean, coordinated woman approached our table, spouting niceties with any whiff of feminine grace, my grandmother would frown at me, somehow rolling her eyes and deadening them at the same time. "What's she so happy about, Joey?" my grandmother would whisper—often when "she" was still within earshot. My grandmother had bred in my mother this same contempt. When I was a kid, my mother disparaged my few friends' moms, saying she wasn't one of those "smiley, crafty, fake, nicey-nice people."

By people, she meant women. She was fine with nicey-nice men.

Looking back, I had recast that misogyny as a critique of ditzy unseriousness. Perhaps because I was not praised for physical attractiveness, as early as first grade I thought of myself as an artist. You're not so cautious about donning mantles when you're young. I'd had every reason to believe I would be an artist: my free time was devoted to private painting and sculpture classes the way other girls' was to ballet or tap; I read biographies of (male) Impressionists; I made a sixty-page book of drawings called *Girls and Mermaids*. I was suspicious of fun with no artistic end and sensed that the Barbie-dress-up-Pretty-Pretty-Princess fun pandered to girls was worst of all. Indeed, Linda Nochlin writes, the "voice of the feminine mystique, with its potpourri of ambivalent narcissism and internalized guilt . . . subtly dilutes and subverts that inner confidence, that absolute certitude and self-determination (moral and ethic), demanded by the highest and most innovative work in art."

My mother used to buy me a molding clay called Marblex. It smelled earthy and damp. It came in an obdurate gray lump that you had to knead and work to form into a giving mass. Once you shaped the clay, you waited days for it to harden. Then you could paint your basket of flowers or your seal or your woman in a hoop skirt.

My body became that malleable clay when I developed anorexia. Starving myself made self-transformation into a work of conceptual art, played out on a suburban, seventh-grade stage. The more weight I lost—fifteen, twenty, twenty-five, thirty pounds—the more my body seemed to match my creative mind. This new mind–body union made me skeptical of the worldview espoused by my mother and grandmother. Perhaps they envied women whose bodies were attractive. Perhaps their frustrations with age or weight were symptoms of deeper frustrations with their lack of agency. Perhaps they were rebelling against the gender roles they had been conditioned to adopt. Perhaps all of that sustained their negativity.

At fifteen, I had a mental breakdown in the middle of Mexico. I fell into a deep depression, and my skepticism turned into abhorrence back home. I hated being down. I hated my apathy toward schoolwork. I hated sleeping all day and struggling to take a shower, and I hated, once I was in the shower, willing myself to leave. I felt weak, depleted, and docile as a drugged puppy. Sleepily I watched my mother and grandmother take out their discontent on the people around them—children, spouses, deli lady at Jewel, manager at Marshall Field's. I hated that, too. It was wrong. It had consequences.

One unexpected consequence was it made me try to become kind. In front of my mother or my grandmother, I weaponized this kindness; with teachers, counselors, my boss at the hardware store, I tried to effect soft-spoken, deferential grace. Also, I made writing my North Star. If I stayed focused on my purpose, I would never be like them.

And yet, like the white paint flaking off our kitchen wall and revealing mint green underneath, I saw signs that I had become what I'd worked so hard to avoid. The university where I taught, a Catholic women's school, advertised with stock photos of teenage girls and a single purple word: *Unstoppable.* Every time a bus chugged by with one of those ads on its side, I thought, *Gag me.* The doctrine of maternal (spending) power pandered by Goop and digital media was just as bad. All of it keeping women trapped in a materialistic narcissism that would divert resources—the most valuable, of course, being time and capital—from any significant work.

This was why I needed Agnes Martin. She embodied positivity and receptiveness to innocence and beauty that had been missing in my mother and grandmother, and combined with not just do-it-yourself faith but do-it-yourself identity, directed toward making lasting art. That she renounced the shiny trappings of femininity in the process only made her, in my eyes, more badass.

Yet here I was, fawning at the neck dance of a bouncy baby girl. Eating oozy cheese. Batting my eyes, swaying to George Michael.

Exclamation mark on heart.

Cube on infant-crawling-into-*Homo-sapiens*.

Cube on pink.

Cube on hourglass.

————

At the first gallery on Bent Avenue, the candles smelled like leather. The proprietor was from Dallas. He was sun-red after a morning at Taos Pueblo: he'd taken a Texan friend and heard the tour for about the fiftieth time.

"Honestly I could practically give the tour by now," he told us. "Oldest documented settlement, that's one thousand years. Documented."

He led us to works by Pueblo artists. In one interview, Martin said that, as a student in New Mexico, she'd painted "the Indians." Later, I would learn, when she first settled on the mesa, she had walked and walked with a Native chief.

While we regarded photorealist black-and-white oils and sculptures the color of gourds, the proprietor left to greet a former employee, his accent filling in the gaps between the art.

"The fish," I heard him say, "are selling very well."

My husband and I wandered. In a back room, two long tables served up books by and about New Mexican artists.

"Look!" My husband brushed my shoulder, pointing at a paperback of the Princenthal biography. "Agnes Martin!"

I felt a weird combination of defensive, pathetic, and trapped, like when my mother told me she'd read something I'd written. Was this table, finally/only now, validating my work in his eyes? Didn't he recognize? The cover was the same as the dust jacket on the hardback I'd been schlepping around. Agnes Martin, big-eyed, plaintive, smocked, looked up at me: What are you doing in a frou-frou gallery when you could be in your studio?

"That's the one I read," I said.

We retraced our steps to the other end of the gallery. The floor was loud. In this room, the burnished brass frames were better than the art. The paintings were obvious and senti-mental, moody with holy light, subjects the insipid offspring of Mary Cassatt and Edward Hopper: a moony woman in a field staring off toward another moony woman in another field abandoning her hens for another moony woman in an-other field dressed in we're-not-in-Kansas-anymore ging-ham, gripping a basket, glum, hunched, sensing the world as she knew it was about to be twistered away. The artist was attempting to capture states of coming apart, and the whole series depressed me with its jouissance-less view of female suffering.

The proprietor appeared in the doorway again like a smug

cat. He caught me mid-wither, a hand over my belly blocking the baby from the overwrought daubs.

He had a waxy smile. "Still doing all right?"

My husband responded. I breathed toward the exit. The proprietor must've seen. He widened his stance, toes parallel with the lintel.

"So," he said, hands on his hips. "When are you due?"

"October," I said somberly.

"And how are you feeling?"

"Good," I said. I glanced at the wall of paintings and rolled my eyes. "Good."

The left corner of his mouth lifted. Sassy eyebrow. He looked at my husband. He looked at me. He looked at my husband. "Really? How about you?"

Outside the fragrant gallery, my husband appeared elated.

"That's the first time someone's asked me how I'm doing," he said. He sounded surprised and appreciative, almost revived.

I nodded. "How did it feel, to be asked how you're doing?"

I listened and tried to be attentive.

So you're huge, I told myself as we walked. I shrunk behind my sunglasses. Strangers saw me as a mother: not a woman, not a writer. In the second volume of *My Struggle*, in which Karl Ove Knausgård struggles with raising his children, there's a line about the neutering, self-erasing aspect of being a parent—"the leveling," he writes, is what enrages him, the "[forfeiting] everything that was me." I related to that, and I wasn't even really a parent yet. In Bentonville, the owner of

Ozark Mountain Bagel had asked me how I was doing, when I was due, if the heat was zapping me. In Oklahoma City, a custodian paper-toweling sinks in the women's restroom at the restaurant we'd gone to for brunch had hustled out, mid-wipe. "No, no," she'd said. "Can't make a pregnant lady wait. All yours." I wasn't cultivating any particularly literary mien—my husband used our *New Yorker* tote—but I still hoped some bookish/astute aspect of my comportment would signal *writer*, the true me.

Alas—

There was an arcade adjacent to Bent Avenue. Bedding shops, man-sandal shops, Italian suit shops, Life Is Good terrycloth shops. We stopped at Op Cit Books. The shingle out front: typewriter font, excessive kerning, an eyesight chart on the cinchiest line.

Inside, we browsed New and Used. Apart from a trio of older women holding takeout cartons, we were the only customers.

"We have an upstairs and a dollar rack in back," the clerk at the register called.

I wondered if being paycheck-to-paycheck in debt was as obvious as pregnancy to rich people. Her saying that made me feel ashamed of myself. What was I doing away from my desk when I had negative money?

I could feel the clerk watching me. I glanced toward the register and smiled, trying to assure her that I wasn't going to steal a book.

She was looking at me and looking through me. Her hair

was a jagged crop. She wore fine-framed neutron-blue glasses. "Feel free to sit down if you need to."

I picked up *The Country Life* and turned to the About the Author flap, forcing myself to absorb the ridiculous bounty of Rachel Cusk's youthful vitae.

"Ma'am!" The clerk shouted now, pointing her voice. "Ma'am! Feel free to sit!"

I looked up, hunting for the older women who'd been in the store a second ago. I looked for crutches, a cast, one of those black braces people call boots. Then I met the clerk's eyes. She was talking to me.

"You. Miss. Pregnant Person."

I put down the book. I wanted to tell the woman she was mistaken: I wasn't pregnant, simply fat, strangely fat, all the adiposity lumped on my front. I wanted to tell her she was mistaken. I wanted to be like Agnes Martin, mistook for a man and puckish about it.

"I'm ready to go," I told my husband. "I'll meet you out front."

I glared behind my sunglasses as I passed the clerk.

"Do you need any water?" she shouted.

———

I went to the public bathroom, a door down a corridor smashed between shops. In the streaky mirror, I stared at every part of me that wasn't my body. Sunglasses, hair, gold hoop earrings, rings. I did one hundred tricep pushbacks facing a hair dryer grungy with stickers.

Where had the hot louche moments of pregnancy gone? I thought back to brunch in Oklahoma City, how that morning we'd woken up in an immense industrial-loft four-room suite in the 21c Hotel ("Lady Gaga just stayed there," the front desk clerk had boasted, upgrading our standard king), and I'd told my husband to find me on the couch. The curtains were open, tinted shades covered the enormous windows, muffling everything in shadow. It was still dark when he pushed me against a wall and nosed between my legs. I shut my eyes and stuck out my ass. His mouth on my neck. His tongue on my spine. I pressed my hands against the wall. My pulse came in my palms. I moved us to the daybed, he lifted my legs straight in the air, licked me, spread me. I said do you like to eat me out—eat me, empty me, gut me, swallow me, take me out of myself. Then the good woozy swim of being fucked when you've already orgasmed. The more pregnant I got, the harder I wanted him to fuck me, the more I liked him yanking my hair, cranking my neck, throttling me, putting his fingers in my mouth, fucking me so hard I heard his penis become a cock. Ruin me, destroy me, I used to think when we were trying to get me pregnant, his semen flooding my body with its bleachy perfume. Now I wanted him to fuck the baby out like he'd fucked the baby in.

And yet, maybe sex had deluded me. Tricked me into thinking pregnancy had its perks. "After you make love, you're just so dumb," says Martin. She describes sex as "fifteen minutes of physical abrasion."

12.

"BEAUTIFUL DAY!" THE FOURTH man said.

"Beautiful!" I said a fourth time.

The rain had burned off. Lucy was at the casita. It was late morning when my husband and I got to the trailhead. We were finally hiking Divisadero. Martin's walkabouts hadn't been confined to New York. She'd walked acres of northern New Mexico, alone and with friends, and I believed that had been part of her process, making art, because I believed you had to make all of life part of your process. Now I was taking a proper hike—pregnancy wouldn't stop me.

A few days ago, we'd set out to hike Divisadero.

It was a distracting morning. Don't listen to dog, don't feel dejected, don't feel adrift, don't feel lonely, don't feel insecure, don't feel fat, don't feel pregnant, don't read—you should be writing, don't write—you should be reading, don't go on-line to look for a hike, don't find a hike, don't look up a translation of the name ("divisadero," to gaze upon from a distance), don't check email, don't check bank account, don't invite husband to gaze upon from a distance.

But I had gone on the internet. I'd given myself ten min-utes to pick a reasonable hike. Ten minutes had turned to fifteen, and then I was in email—emails, three for three dif-ferent jobs, plus my personal account.

The trailhead was a five-minute drive from the casita. My husband brought water. Water, leash, Lucy. The guilt of breaking a rule after abandoning my work was a passenger in the car. I stretched the seat belt. I had the mounting sense that I was doing everything wrong: writing, studying Agnes Martin, being in Taos, being pregnant.

When we parked and looked at the trail maps, Divisadero was too long, my husband decided. Better Ojitos: one mile, flattish. Little eye.

"I want to get back to work," my husband said.

"Sure," I mumbled.

We crossed a footbridge that shelved us on the South Boundary Trail and branched off, up a small switchback that ascended toward a modest view. The Río Don Fernando was

below us, trickling, foaming, spilling over onto the rocks.
Hissing.

Only I barely saw any of it. I was so angry with myself.
Perhaps it was the nature of residencies or vacations for them
to be dead time; perhaps I'd been delusional, expecting to get
to Taos and have epiphanies left and right. My eyes wouldn't
focus. I felt like I was going to erupt.

While my husband watched Lucy graze on clover, I stood
by a bench carved with initials. Chiseled in the wood, it was
clear that letters were lines. I thought about all those tiny
vertical lines in *Milk River*—what if they had been hundreds
of little *I*s? Is this what it took for me to have an insight?
Hanging back a few feet, getting absorbed in a solid material
form? I imagined ditching them, running off into the pines;
without water, I would faint eventually. When I awoke, I
would find the river and forage, or a bear would devour me,
or I'd squat for three months until the baby shot out.

I took a few steps forward, looking out at the mountains,
three blue-purple stripes. I picked up Lucy and showed her
the panorama, too. I wanted so badly to feel good.

"She's looking," I said, amazed. "She doesn't always do
this."

"She is," my husband said. "She's taking it in."

I tried to take it in, too. A pinecone-brown lizard ran
through the brush. Tall stalks tipped in yellow at my back.
The trail dropped and split. One way led to the water.

Eventually, we'd sat on the rocks at the river's edge, tucked
in this wooded alcove. The stream was clear. The water licked

my wrist. Hand in neon algae, bearding off the rocks, a mossy flame. Gold Gila trout grazing my fingers. The band of blush on its belly told me it was spawning.

———

Now, we were devoting our day to the hike. We were on Divisadero's six-mile loop. For the first time in a long time, I felt strong. I was twenty-nine weeks pregnant and putting on many altitudinous steps.

On our first switchback, we passed a woman whose silver hair was tied back in a low ponytail. She had a lean, Jane Goodall body. She shot a smile at me and asked how I was doing.

"Good!" I crowed.

"How's the baby?"

"Good!"

"Good for you!"

My first instinct was to translate the exchange: Aww, poor dumpy mother, here's a gold star for perambulating. Then I remembered Suzuki's swinging door and let that door bump my translation right off the cliff. I was concentrating on keeping my footing, observing the trees and the flowers and the dirt, the way every turn seemed to take us to another biome, lauding myself: This is easy. You're not out of breath. This is difficult and you're doing it. Good for you. You're a champ. You're nothing. Your body reminds you what you're capable of. Your body is not your work. Your husband should be proud. Your husband shouldn't let you do this. Should pregnant women hike? This hike is nothing. You should hike more. Your husband is annoyed. You're talking too much. Martin would have done this. No. Martin would've hiked alone. No. Martin had done that canoeing trip. No, she had hiked with friends. Hiking, camping, being in nature—some of the best times, she said somewhere. Did she think she was neglecting her work? If she has time to hike, I have time to hike. No, I'm different, I don't have her vision, I need to work harder. I'm working hard enough. I'm nothing.

We paused to take our photo, where the rocks were velveteen with neon moss. I tried to look cheerful and thought, *Viridescent.*

"I think people are more sensitive to your pregnancy in Taos," my husband said.

I'm more sensitive to my pregnancy in Taos, I thought.

I shrugged. "It's been nonstop since Arkansas. I must've . . . popped."

I could see my popping in the picture. I wore a baseball cap and sunglasses, leggings, a small backpack to offset my belly, an old T-shirt, and my navel poked through the cotton. The T-shirt had been my mother's: she wore it when I was a baby, when she was young and a babe, by my father's account, fun-loving and happy. The cotton was soft, pale blue, tissue thin. On the front, a sketch of a filigreed lamppost and a mansion white as meringue, bandwagon font: *New Orleans.*

My husband and I walked through dry desert patches of scabby earth and the lush umbrage of evergreens, through wide aisles of trail and up narrow passes, lapsing in and out of conversation, pausing to take small mouthfuls of tinny water. Just before we reached the peak, we found a clear patch on the sloping ground off the trail. We looked between the skinny pine trunks, out over the whole valley.

Soon, the summit seemed close. We sat on the loam. I took out a white paper bag from the backpack. We'd stopped in town before heading to the trail and bought vegetable sandwiches from Manzanita. Sweet roasted yellow peppers and mashed avocado, turmeric hummus, frilly lettuce, sprouts of clover on soft wheat bread.

We unwrapped the sandwiches and ate. The earth was padded with fir needles and fine dirt. We were eating slowly, but it felt like gorging, stuffing myself, delicious and breathless. We'd climbed thirteen hundred feet in the last two hours.

Quiet. The sandwich, the slope of the cliff, the enormity of the view, the world below and surrounding us. Agnes Martin's sky. This air, these colors. The concerns I'd had on our ascent seemed to vanish. This sandwich was delicious. I felt still and focused. At the gate of emptiness. My knees were tented. I turned a doorknob and entered a solitude. A lonely, uninhabited place. As in: wilderness, wilds, backwoods, the sticks, backveld, middle of nowhere; emptiness, wasteland, retirement, desert.

This will end, I thought, and that will be all right.

I will be all right.

We finished and walked on. I kept peeking over my shoulder for bears and only saw a white weasel with a swanky tail.

———

From then on, I decided to let my experiment progress more naturally. I was trying too hard, forcing the whole solitude thing.

I turned on my phone the next morning. I was in the kitchen, boiling water for tea, listening to a neighbor's guitar amping up, when the paper tag of my tea bag caught fire off the burner. I dumped water over the mug and heard the singe.

I could still smell smoke in the spare bedroom. I climbed up to the top bunk, reclined on the pillows and stretched out my legs long, pretending I was condemned to sniff the ceiling, tossing my phone like a hacky sack. Not watching porn. It would've been so easy to watch porn. Even to get off on the thought of watching porn. Would time be engorged until I let myself go/come? Perhaps this was the reset I needed, or—

A bird drew three long ascending notes, then four fast barbed chirps. The shadows of the sagebrush tapered like gray flames. The shabby tangle of roots and branches, the wide reach of broad leaves, blue green silver, pointy as church palms.

I climbed down and put on my shoes.

A few blocks from the casita, I called my mother.

"Are you walking on a highway?" she asked. "What's that noise?"

"Traffic. It's a road."

"You better be careful. You're pregnant, Missy."

. . .

"Are you overexerting yourself?"

I felt, then, the awful patheticness of my time here. The

desperate attempt to become . . . better. To matter. To do something meaningful, serious, to make something bigger than myself—wasn't this what Martin meant when she talked about painting universal emotions? I wanted my mother to ask me about my research, to remember the name Agnes Martin, to ask me about New Mexico—or at least to discipline me (inspire me), tell me to go back to my room, do my work, get off the phone, turn off the phone (wasn't that what I'd promised her and the rest of my family and my friends, no contact for three weeks?), use this time concertedly. She never would've prodded me like that.

Yet, in a way, I liked what she asked me, too. I liked how she thought me high risk; when I felt bemused by my whole, dull, depressoid adult existence, I even liked that she talked over me, talked at me, ignored what was important to me, chided me, making light of what I did or didn't eat, because it proved I was over it, the years of hurt. When I tried to describe the nature of that hurt, I could not. Emotional hurt, that's as far as I got. I couldn't explain what it had been like to grow up with her. I came up with odd bits and pieces, the murky, monochromatic middle pieces of a puzzle, none of the frame: A sweaty day in April, sophomore year in high school: Her suspicion enflamed when I came downstairs wearing a long-sleeved T-shirt with my miniskirt, she'd tackled me to the orange linoleum in the kitchen, pinned me with a knee, yanked up my sleeves, bellowing and wailing at my pathetic safety-pin cuts: so minor, compared to my friend's work with a blade. I'd scrambled away. Get over here, JoAnna. Get the fuck over here. Mom, calm down, you're overreacting, these are old, these are minor, let me call my therapist. Get the fuck over here now. I'd called 911. Before college, the night of my first overdose: I'd asked a friend's mom to drive me to the ER; I'd spent twelve hours on an IV, ears sirening, refusing to give staff permission to tell my mother where I was, and I'd spent four days in the psych ward without allowing her to visit. All the guilt and shame I felt around her for having problems (dealing with an eating disorder, dealing with her trying to control how I dealt with an eating disorder). The daily machinations of the hurt were so hard to recall, I wondered if I'd blocked it out, especially when friends marveled at our closeness now, at "what a big person" I was for getting over that kind of treatment, when they knew how it had been.

The sun was warming my arms and shoulders. "I'm just taking a break—just taking a walk around the house."

I wanted her to be curious about my work. Even with all the prevaricating I seemed to be doing, I was making progress. I'd written sixty text blocks in the last week. I didn't care if they were awful: I just wanted to be doing the work, and I was doing the work, and the amassment of work was maybe proof I had no reason to question my interest in Agnes Martin or my ability to write about her or even my desire to semi-live like her, semi-be her. I wanted my mother to ask me about anything but the baby or my body (which belonged to the baby); instead, she began talking about herself. The pool overrun with kids. She was tired of the health club. She was on her way for a soft serve. Finally, she seemed to remember I was there.

"How many steps do you walk? Do you measure the miles? I guess what I'm trying to say is how do you clock it?"

I didn't. Sometimes, I told her weakly, I checked the time when I left and when I returned. I thought, I'm not concerned about not being concerned. I'd been struck by Suzuki: "If you are not concerned about what you do, you will not say so." My professor had drawn a line beside this passage. "When you sit, you will sit. When you eat, you will eat."

"Oh." My mother sounded disappointed. "I'm always just interested in the steps."

———

Razor wire braided into the big sagebrush, teeth glinting in the argent leaves. A nip of Fireball in the albino dirt, the fevered dancer pounding his feet on the label, faded from the sun. Everything etherized in dust, shimmering, washed away in the wake of a blue car speeding down Weimer. A dandelion species as big as a Santa Barbara sea urchin.

I cupped my hand around the sphere and held the word *sprung* before I took off.

I was running. I ran from Henning Drive and the baby didn't come tumbling out. Fifteen minutes in, I paused. Heat-thick breath. Hands on my waist. I stared at an empty lot.

Lion-colored grasses, masses of wildflowers. I hadn't picked a flower in years. This week, the baby was as big as two bunches of kale. I felt good and strong, or I was determined to feel good and strong.

It'll come back, I whispered, hiding the words under my tongue like I'd once done with multivitamins.

We've got this, I told the baby boy.

I was only winded when I stopped and saw:

a bug, an arrowhead, hissing in the brush;

pinyon-junipers greening the hillside;

showy yellow cinquefoil. Search "cacti."

Search "white," "leafless," "yuccas."

Wild strawberries, mountain death camas, tawny cryptantha, sweet four o'clock, Arizona valerian, member of the honeysuckle family—small-petaled, conspiring.

13.

FOR ONCE THE SKY WAS UNAS-
tonishing: overcast, sewage gray, flat.
The plaza was in front of us. On
our right was a gallery and a boutique real-estate brokerage. On our
left was a hut selling bottles of soda
and dried-red-chile everything: dan-
gling bouquets, wreaths, corsages and
boutonnières and doorknob bracelets.
Red chile, I'd later learn, was a Pueblo
apotropaic against evil spirits.

We were on our way back to the
museum. Having seen Martin's paintings alone, it was safe to bring my
husband. I felt oddly possessive. Now
his presence wouldn't overshadow my
response to the work.

On our short drive to the museum, I could've told him how the color he was about to see in the seven paintings in the gallery was characteristic of her post-mesa work, or how a condition of the installation was that the work would never travel: Martin's emphasis on the permanent exhibit. I could've talked about how a desire for permanence took me back to being thirteen, watching the crucible of a sunset out my bedroom window and crying with my whole body, realizing that one day my mother and my father and my brother and my sister would die—that I would die. A childish or childlike thought? Childish an insult, childlike a padded compliment. No, no adjectives. Only nouns. A child's thought. A vein of childhood ran through Martin's work, I could've said, preparing him for the gentle blues in the gallery, quoting "The Current of the River of Life Moves Us": "Inspiration like a good mother returns." If you're not possessed of a good mother, conjure your own.

Instead, I spoke about suicide. Suicide and life insurance— so scintillating it'd push anyone over the brink.

"Did you know you wouldn't get life insurance if I committed suicide?" I said. "Doesn't that seem wrong?"

My husband's forehead bunched. And yet I was committed to walking this tightrope over the lion pit. Ladies and gentlemen, boys and girls, what will she say next?

"It's just so arbitrary. A person can smoke themselves stupid, pretty much aim for lung cancer, die of that, and their family gets money. If you're depressed, and in pain, and you've tried everything else, and you want to—"

My voice caught. For once I wanted him to agree with me about death.

"JoAnna, you're scowling." My husband's hands lay lightly on the steering wheel. Ready to flail in exasperation. Or grab my wrist. Or lock the doors.

"What? Why isn't that valid?"

I felt spiteful and mean. I imagined my mind a clock without numbers, stick arms, maniacally windmilling. That morning, I'd been paid. I'd transferred most of my paycheck to a credit card. I'd filled six-inch squares of text with writing five times. I'd made myself write those five squares without backtracking. I said what I was trying to say more clearly. Not quite. I tried to figure out what I was trying to say. I heard a sound. I tried again. I searched for stars I drew next to quotes I needed to use. E.g., Martin telling Jill Johnston: "It's forever raining when the sun is shining." A reminder that she acknowledged pain and beauty, suffering and happiness. I'd drawn arrows and stars.

I had a plan for the day: I would go back to the Harwood by myself.

But then I hadn't wanted to be lonely, and I was lonely, so I'd invited my husband, out of weakness—I was tired of subjecting myself to solitude—and guilt—didn't he deserve to go to the museum, too? After inviting him, I'd prevaricated and frustrated him.

(I must have frustrated him—I'd frustrated myself.)

"Are we going or am I getting back to work?" he'd asked.

"You can go," I'd said sullenly.

"I'm only going if I'm going with you," he'd said.

Fine. Fine.

I recognized my contradictions; they were too much. I didn't want to be seen as pregnant and I didn't want the invisibility of pregnancy. I hated the exceptionalism of pregnancy and I hated that in October I'd file for "disability" on account of pregnancy to take maternity leave. I hated the idea of a leave. You're going to want the time, cherish it, people said. My internal retorts were paranoid and vicious: Why, so my writing is derailed? So I'm lulled into a getting-by mindset wherein I congratulate myself for keeping up with emptying the diaper pail? So no one has to see the ruins of an inflated body? Yet in moments I might describe as the peaks of pregnancy—so peak, they evaporated into the clouds—I felt honed, awake, primed to notice everything. The churn of a generator cycling on, the disjointed symphony of birds' glissando behind the curtains, the *thwk* of my eyelashes when I blinked. The cool bondage of slipping on my grandmother's diamond ring for this excursion, the double-hitch of diamonds snicking fabric. I could change for the better. Perhaps carrying a child, I'd already grown more aware. Slowed down. More cautious, and in this cautiousness, aware of a world I'd otherwise miss—a world bigger than myself.

That morning, a rabbit had caught my eye out the window, when I was turned away from my work. I'd watched it pick through the backyard, perch on rocks, nibble the twiggy shrubs. The rabbit was compact yet rangier than the rabbits that paused on our lawn in Illinois. This rabbit ate for a minute. Then a truck rumbled down Weimer Road and the rabbit sprang, its small body stretched like a nylon.

Why couldn't I see pregnancy as an occasion for this awareness, for inspiration, for adventure? Why couldn't I treat it like Martin leaving New York, going forward into unknown territory?

Except, what was I leaving and where was I leaving from and how long would I have to drive before my vision of adobe brick?

All this had made the cumbrous matter of whether to bring my husband to the Harwood worse: he would see how stupid I was with Martin's paintings, gawping in front of them, wowie kazowie (when, what, I should be levitating?), and he'd be there with his Moleskine, writing cogent cursive while I darkened the gallery with my bad mood.

In the car, I glared at the chiles, polished and leathery. I thought: *Stuff my corpse with red chiles.*

"JoAnna." My husband sounded angry. "Hello? I said you're scowling."

"If I killed myself," I said, "I'd want you and the baby to get the money. I'd be doing it so you could live life without the burden of me. If I were in such a bad headspace . . ."

"Why have you been researching this?"

The light changed. My husband inched, waiting for Plaza traffic so he could turn left.

I told him a story someone had recently told me. A friend's ex-husband was found dead in bed in his condo, Mother's Day weekend. The place was a sty. Faded *Sun-Times*

in brown grocery bags. One of his adult children discovered the body; there was an investigation. The man had a
heart condition. Depression. Some suspicion about a bottle
of lotion on a nightstand, and the lotion was under analy-
sis. Suspicion turned stuff into evidence. Evidence would
dictate outcome—in this case, whether the man's insurance
would or would not dispense life insurance money. The ex-
wife was upset on many levels. The divorce had never been
official. She could use the money. The adult children could
use the money.

"Why insurance should care how you die is so moralizing
and gross," I said.

My husband's eyes left the road. He looked right at me.
"Do you want me to commit suicide?"

Of all the stupid responses, I thought.

"No! Why would you say that?"

He didn't get it. Suicide was mine, my trip, my raft to float
away on, my ferry to the isle of null. But first I wanted the
baby to be born healthy and safe. I wanted to hold the baby.
Then I'd know it would be better for him if I were gone.

"Just checking."

He reminded me about the new life insurance policy he'd
taken out when we found out I was pregnant. If, by sixty-five,
he hadn't died, we could withdraw the money like any other
401(k). We pulled into the museum parking lot, and he went
on explaining the perks.

———

The Harwood had once been a private estate called El Pueblito. Later, it was Taos's first library. The space had a quiet studiousness: floors of supple, haptic wood suited to ballerinas practicing ronds de jambe; walls the color of garlic papers; around this or that corner, a steep staircase and vaulted ceilings.

I could see light from a bank of windows at the end of the corridor that led to the Agnes Martin Gallery. My husband and I stood at the gift shop ticketing window. There wasn't a question: we would each go through the museum, alone.

"Find me whenever you're ready," he said. "Take as long as you want. JoAnna." He took my hand, deadweight. "I know you're struggling today, and I love you."

I stared at my espadrilles, half-lifted my head, and watched his sandaled feet walk off.

For a moment, I marveled at him. How was he so forgiving, so patient? How could he so plainly label it? You're struggling. From time to time, I could muster that kind of utterance, but more often I could only sense there was something wrong and whatever that something was was seriously compromising my ability to exist. My mind was ragged and disobedient, unwilling to concentrate; I was alternately adrenalized with rage and torporific—I felt leaden and stuck, like a shoe swallowed by mud; my entire body seemed to give off an aura, the emanating throb of an analgesic-advertisement wound.

Even my diagnoses du jour (dysthymia and maybe fat-pregnant me would still score an EDNOS) sounded horridly manageable and tame compared to how awful I felt. I

often wished for migraines to accompany my depression, for
the comfort of a symptom.

I went down the long corridor, toward the Martin Gallery, and stopped at the neighboring exhibit. There was a
recession, a dark alcove, and a pink satin kneeler, with a sign
that said, PLEASE DO NOT TOUCH.

This was Ken Price's *Death Shrine I*. I read the object labels
before looking at the installation. I was attracted to the mix of
material and immaterial language in those descriptions. Ernest Gombrich, in *The Sense of Order*: "Looking at an object
is not the same as scanning our environment for order . . .
There must be a conflict, or at least a tension, between the
two forms of perception . . . the perception of things and the
perception of order." I liked that tension. Applied to Price's
work, for instance, the phrase *relaxed concentration*.

On a bench in front of the kneeler, I tried to relax into
concentration, taking in Price's garish world. Spotlights shone
on a white and turquoise picket fence. The fence hedged in
a snug tableau of skull stuff: memento mori meets kitsch. A
little domestica played out in orange fringe and sateen, an al-
tarpiece with droves of grinning skeletons painted on saucers
and plates, silver vases teeming with ferns. There was Victo-
rian wallpaper (all flu-gray roses) and an acrylic of happy skeletons hauling a coffin. There were skulls on tchotchkes and
skulls on mugs, skulls on tablecloths and skulls in stained-glass
hangings, a clutter of skulls on plates. I could hear my breath,
weak as basting thread, straining for the eye of a needle.

———

Later, back at the casita, after we had sex on the couch, my forehead smashed into the arm of the cushions, after I came and the rattle in my brain stopped, I stood outside. A wind surged through the field, a wave in the encroaching dark, sloughing over the land, lanterns and porch lights beaming on sensor, close up, in the distance—*coruscating*.

Words like that infiltrated my thinking. I saw the rise and dips of the horizon, and thought back to the pressed cool of the museum, to the preverbal peace I felt looking at Martin's art. She made everything seem simple. This was one of her gifts. She painted straight lines and there were not straight lines in nature, she said, so she couldn't be painting nature. I wanted to undo my vocabulary. I wanted simpler.

I could affect the complexity of the pleasure I received with my mouth: by opening my mouth quite vertically, over my husband's neck or his chin, my breath became something hot to swallow, or barely scraping my teeth against his flesh, grazing the jut of his chin, with my mouth, I could catch the edge of a cliff and keep myself suspended, an ache in the cove of the underarm, fingers curling, my mouth held on, trying to clench and unclench, a coil of pleasure wound around my whole body when I tipped my head, arched my neck, waiting to orgasm (senior year of high school: Bernini's St. Teresa in ecstasy protected in packing tape on my notebook cover), I liked pleasure to be a strickening, a succumbing, and I succumbed harder with a cock in my mouth, a different state of expansion, a horizontal fullness, a fuller fullness; otherwise, I chewed a pillow or bit my own arm.

(I filled my mouth so I would not hear myself whimpering like a whelp, *whelp* being first a verb and then a noun: 1] the act of a dog giving birth or 2] a puppy.)

I stood at the side door. The wind whipped through tall grasses and bent bare branches. I was listening for transformation. The religious kiss crosses, thumb their breviaries, lick the earth. Lifting my hair and cracking my neck, showing my ears, flaunting my throat, yes, cocking my head like a dog's.

Soon the yips surrounded me. In the plots of land abutting the mountains, coyotes loped through the dust, vanishing into scrub.

———

A few steps from the Price, an entire corridor was devoted to Judy Chicago. I stood in front of *Mother India*, reading Chicago's statement—"Investigation of Birth"—feeling like an exhibit prop, carted out with belly and maternity romper.

When I'd first seen Chicago's *Dinner Party*, the grainy slide projector images of it, back in high school Art History, I'd hated its flagrant feminism. All those bone china beavers and boxes. That hate saddened me. Now, I was extra glad for Judy Chicago. I was not ludicrous or histrionic: there was global precedent for being negated by baby.

In my notebook, I wrote: "Many countries keep no records of maternal mortality, as the mother's experience is not considered important, only the infant's."

"You're welcome to take photos," the tall guard said. "Just no flash. If you don't want to scribe this all down."

"I didn't bring a phone," I said.

The guard had a large bearish nose; the follicles of what once must've been sandy eyebrows; a carved, weather-beaten quality.

"Or a camera," he offered.

He was lingering and I walked away. *Mother India* was the gateway to *Birth Project*, an exhibit that consumed nearly half of the Harwood's first floor. Maybe I would look at the rest if I had time after sitting with the Martins.

There was no one in the Agnes Martin Gallery, and I sat on one of the square stools. I faced *Untitled (Playing)*. Looking this time, I noticed what she was doing with colors: the slightest difference in saturation or hue allowed one painting to distinguish itself from the next. *(Playing)* was the bluest of the canvases: washed blue bands bisected by white belts, bordered by darker blues. I thought of what I'd recovered in my notebook, what Martin had told Johnston, about forever raining and the sun shining. The variations in a single tone—lighter and darker blue—reminded me of that metaphorical weather.

Somewhere, the security guard was talking about photorealism. Streaming in through the oculus, the dim July sun hit Martin's graphite lines so they seemed deeper, penetrating, razored across the paintings. Only I wasn't thinking about those lines—I was thinking about life insurance and debt. If I could kill myself without it seeming obvious I'd killed myself, after the baby was born; perhaps my husband could get the life insurance on me and stop worrying about debt. Not just my credit card. My husband's credit card, too.

I looked down. I'd stopped taking notes.

I tried to bring myself back. I counted the horizontal lines and the different widths of horizontal lines, and tried to name the pattern, but the tranquility of the space was broken. The whole task seemed effortful and arbitrary. Better the snowy vanishment of *Untitled (Innocence)* to its left? No. I sat still, pretending I was not thinking what I was thinking. I got up.

Outside the gallery, I glanced at Martin's *Nude.* Some critics believe it depicts a partner; others nod to the bone structure, the cheekbones, the resemblance to Agnes. If it is her, she's all torso with ample breasts; she wears chunky bangs and glinting earrings: a woman borrowed from Gauguin. When Martin visited the Harwood, I'd read, early work like this was taken down to keep her from vandalizing it.

———

I cut through the room with the fireplace; then I was amid *Birth Project.*

"Did you get a gallery guide?" said an old woman, hair in a bun like a portobello cap.

"Oh, I'm okay."

She looked annoyed. "Because they're out. They're supposed to be right here."

Was she too lazy to read? In the Mandelman–Ribak Gallery, writing was part of the project: paragraphs outnumbered textiles ten to one. I felt myself buck up.

Birth Project was a collaboration on an enormous scale. Chicago organized hundreds of craftswomen and seamstresses and patternmakers, knitters and embroiderers and crocheters, working as coequals all over the country—the opposite of Agnes Martin: a network of women helping each other, constructing something universal and particular together. I felt a twinge of perverse glee. Martin would've hated sharing filtered airspace with Chicago's ovarian opus.

The birth garments, Judy Chicago wrote, "[present] a pregnant body that is both passive and powerful, aggressive and entrapped." What this meant was a textile extravaganza, knits and weavings and crochetings and tapestries, some of them more than twice the size of Martin's paintings, all the sewing-bee stuff Martin denounced, despite the glowing statement she'd written about Lenore Tawney.

I didn't want to connect with *Birth Project*. I wanted the elegant invisibility of Martin's pure *Innocence*. And yet looking at *Great American Mother*, the quilting stitches in contrasting colors of DMC floss, I felt a different energy than what I'd felt in front of Martin's paintings that day. The knotting samples, the macrame labia, *Hatching the Universal Egg*, creation myths in linen appliqué, periwinkle, terra-cotta, a rainbow fading into robin's-egg blue, *The Crowning Q89* with its batiks in purples and blues, stillborn colors, off-white feather stitchery, and worst/best the enormous *Birth: Filet Crochet*: an argent, shark-gray vortex of labor, the lightning bolt of a rent vagina. Muslin mock-ups, Polaroids, swatches, an elaborate material chain letter traveling from Wisconsin to California, New Jersey, Illinois. There were stories of Chicago stopping by a sewer's kitchen, chatting at a Formica-top table over bologna sandwiches, Cokes, warm Toll House cookies.

As I moved through *Birth Project*, my mood lifted. I focused. I read. I took eight pages of notes. An hour passed. People came and went from the gallery, clusters of older women, a gallerista leading a mother and two young daughters. There was a chronicle of the evolution of childbirth. Nineteenth-century doctors anesthetizing mothers to make labor easier. I had to guzzle water, I got so queasy, but I was no longer upset.

One of the needlepointer's journal entries said something that stuck with me. She was sewing a piece about vaginal tearing, all maroons and burgundies, blood colors, and she said if she thought about the image as a whole, it would be too painful. So she took it incrementally. Everything was stitch by stitch.

———

Back in the car, worming behind the Plaza, there was the church and the rock tumbling studio and a playground, purple and orange and yellow and blue, pennants and rope bridge and turrets. Kids were pounding across a drawbridge, clambering over the monkey bars, hollering. In the margins, parents stood, arms folded, watching.

"Did you talk much to the security guard?" my husband said.

"Not really," I said.

"I don't know what it is about me, but people just do this with me."

"You have a nice face. You look like you'll listen."

"I appreciate that. So this guard. He came over and started talking to me—I didn't ask him anything—for ten minutes. He knew Agnes Martin."

I looked out the window. We were back on the NO TIME street. This time, I made a wish.

Quietly I hoped our son would inherit my husband's radiant affability. I hoped he would never find himself in a clinical setting, using the phrase *passive suicidality*. I hoped he would never crave the candy-sweet brown-sugar shell on a handful of standard Advil (also, hoped he'd have no appetite for gallows humor and deem them superior to M&Ms). I couldn't decide if I hoped he would never read my writing or if I hoped he would never know the damaged part of me (excisable and arbitrary as a gallbladder), or if I simply hoped I could be better in a new life, all the breadcrumbs of fucked-uppedness I'd dropped along the way gobbled up by birds.

I turned to my husband, wondering if he was wishing on NO TIME, too.

"Well, what did he tell you?" I said.

"I was right outside the gallery, and he said, 'Do you know how much each of these seven paintings in the gallery is worth?'

"And he said, 'There are three others. Three others in this group. One at a museum in New York, two in a private collection . . . If you wanted to sell one of those paintings, you could do it in about a half hour. Wanna know how much they're worth?'

"'How much?'

"'Each painting in this room is worth $7 million. So that room alone is worth $49 million. That's why I have my job. That gallery is worth more than everything else . . . the building and its entire holdings, its entire collection combined. A lot more.

"'I'm a painter and a collector myself. So I know, all artists have their little . . . quirks. Peculiarities. But do you know what's always stuck with me about Agnes Martin?'

"'What?'

"'Well, she never kept a lot of money. When she was alive, one of her paintings would sell, four or five hundred thousand dollars. And what she'd do with the money was immediately buy a piece of minimalist art. Something valuable. Then she'd destroy it.'

"Then he showed me her old paintings. The self-portrait, the other two. In the hallway behind the gallery."

I didn't correct him about the "self-portrait." The 1947 nude. He wasn't wrong. Any portrait of a woman by another woman was a slant self-portrait.

"He told me when the director of the Harwood knew she was coming to the museum—she liked to sit on one specific stool in her gallery—they'd take down those old paintings. Because she hated them so much, they worried she'd actually destroy them, the guard said."

"That I knew," I said.

"He said, 'I don't feel much when I look at those paintings. Do you?'"

——

There weren't only stories and journal entries interwoven in *Birth Project*. There were quotes from literature:

"Am I pushing or dying?" Anaïs Nin.

Nin always had this effect on me: saying something so plain and true I was immediately turned on. If I had known an orgasm would return me to self-possession—on my first visit, I had leaned against a wall, though that was in a gush of emotion, a different shape of arousal.

Sexual arousal is a tipped grid: a net.

Emotional arousal is a parabola: a cradle.

That evening, after I came, I wondered if the baby felt my orgasm. Where my breath had been shallow and agitated, spoiling the day all day, now it was slow and deep. Outside the sun had dropped. The coyotes were quiet. I was sweating on the bed.

Did the baby notice a change in the temperature of his uterine pool? Did the amniotic fluid assume a sudden electrical current? Was he soothed? Did he glance on his own pleasure in my stimulation? I was not worried about disturbing him. I opened *Writings*.

"Our mind asks, 'is this right?' And it answers, 'yes' or 'no.'"

14.

AT EAGLE NEST LAKE, I HEARD prairie dogs. They popped up from their burrows, squealing and cheeping, testing the rain. As a pack their barks were choral and communicative, like madrigals. (From *matricalis*, "maternal or primitive," or *matrix*, as in "breeding female," later "womb.") Their noisy whack-a-mole act was driving Lucy crazy, and my husband held her leash short.

We had just arrived at the state park, and we were following a smudgy path scattered with fishermen around the lake. It had been a good morning. Four hours writing, no phone, Clif Bar at desk, blueberries at desk: all the things. Today I wasn't even trying to be determined, plucky, or—I thought, alarmed by my au naturel misogyny—the kind of woman a man might admire: I was just doing what I knew I needed to do. Today was easy, effortless, nothing, walking, cold mist on my face.

Before we set out, I'd gone walking the road behind the casita. The world magnified when I felt good. I noticed the alternation in the gravel surface, tracks where trucks and cars drove: tulle of tiny stones (fragile grid), patch of smoothness, pebbles, a leveled swath. Like a dry ocean had lapped the sand, working it down and pushing it up. Swallowing. The ocean was never this gray, gray baked with gold. What was? Not the Rio Grande from up high. Gray of seal pups and swaddles, a pigeon's plumage, gray of steam over sluggard freight train chugging through a spell of daylight. When I got back in, I turned to one of Martin's gray paintings. *Untitled #7*, 1992, acrylic on canvas, seventy-two inches by seventy-two inches. Slender shell-gray stripes alternating with wider stripes of darker lead gray. The gray stains the edges; the stripes span the canvas. Five slender stripes, four wider. The color pales midway up, like a sun opening in a mouth.

It was a gray day, and I accepted it. Enough acting doomed to fail. In "Reflections," Martin writes, "To feel insufficient, to experience disappointment and defeat in waiting for inspiration is the natural state of mind of an artist."

———

The rain began to come down thin and hard, pelting Eagle Nest Lake. I did not consider turning back. The fishermen weren't packing up.

For days I'd been looking at Northern New Mexico—the land, the sky, the rocks, the water—a beauty so huge I struggled with words. Often, talking to my husband, I heard myself, gushy and general. Stunning, amazing, unreal, I said, shuffling through a deck of paltry descriptions: that pink that orange that violet sheer.

Today I said nothing. In Agnes Martin's later paintings, she practiced elimination. She left out from the work everything she did not find perfect. Careful. She kept the horizontal line. The translucent washes of color. It reminded me of what Suzuki writes in *Zen Mind, Beginner's Mind*: "Concentration means more freedom. So your effort should be directed at nothing. You should be concentrated on nothing." Even if this put me at cross-purposes with myself (shouldn't I at least be concentrated on Martin?), it seemed important.

The sun was gone, and the rain was coming harder now, spitting on the lake. Keep going, I thought, don't be the person to give up.

"It's nice to walk in this," I called to my husband.

He sighed, exasperated. "No, it's not."

I caught his eye: The walk was over. He was tugging Lucy through rutted-up ground turning to mud. Along the shore, I saw a woman shoulder her fishing rod and hurry toward the parking lot; beside her, a man gathered six trout bunched together like bananas.

Then we were back in the car, driving west, wet dog smell hanging in the humid cab. A few minutes later, the rain stopped. We slowed down approaching a fork in the highway.

"We haven't been to Angel Fire yet," I said. "Let's see it."

We veered and the road began to climb. There was forested wilderness on our right, and on our left the hills were etched with ski slopes. The slopes kinked down from chalets with snow-peak roofs. Ahead of us, the mountains curved, purple and massive. For an instant I wished I could see my body like that, full and permanent, that the baby who would be in my arms in eighty-five days would know a mother who could be inside her own body with acceptance and grace. Growing up, my own mother was always calling herself fat. She'd talk about how many pounds she'd gained with each kid, how her shoe size had gone up a half size after each birth—any woman that hadn't kept on the weight she gained in pregnancy was suspect—and then she'd eat half the bag of Cape Cod chips on the car ride home from Jewel. At one particularly breakthrough therapy session in my earlier twenties, when I was fresh out of inpatient treatment, I'd had the sort of epiphany one waits a decade for: The eating disorder was a revolt against becoming my mother. The eating disorder was my way of mastering this realm of Lady Life to which my mother was helplessly subject.

But where did that epiphany get me? Fifteen years later, a new therapist was telling me that those comments—about her shoe size, about her body—implanted in the child the idea that she was not wanted, that mother indeed resented child. My therapist said a child was always a gift, the child itself was a gift, and a parent rejecting that gift was the sort of wound that never truly healed. I thought of Margaret Martin sending six-year-old Agnes to have her tonsils taken out by herself. I thought about Martin leaving home and never looking back.

I started to say something about the baby, the third trimester, how I wanted to be or not be, the soonness of it all, but my husband was pointing to the sky.

"You see the rain, don't you?" He pointed to a bus-shaped cloud in front of us. "Look underneath it. See the lightning?"

I didn't then I did. He was worried about driving into the storm: Should we turn around? No, I said. We drove toward it. Soon the cloud dissolved, leaving a pale impression in the sky.

———

In 1967, the year Martin left New York and set off in her Dodge pickup (giving "independence a trial," she wrote to Tawney mid-journey), J. A. Baker's *The Peregrine* was published. The book was the product of Baker traversing the marshy Essex coast for ten winters, searching for peregrines. His birdwatching was an end-days quest: with air-polluting agrochemicals thinning the shells of the peregrine's eggs, the species—"pilgrim falcons"—was at risk of extinction. Baker became possessed, trekking by day, recording impressions in a diary by night. Five drafts later, he'd honed each sentence like a blade: "The eye becomes insatiable for hawks."

Baker's book was acclaimed. It remains both a classic of

nature writing and an example of the consciousness-expanding power of putting all your eggs in a single subject's basket. *The Peregrine*'s obsessive focus makes a text highly specific and highly universal—so highly universal, in fact, that reading, my eye, too, becomes insatiable—insatiable for ars poetica moments germane to my study of Martin.

Take this passage from the book's opening section, "Beginnings":

> To be recognized and accepted by a peregrine you must wear the same clothes, travel by the same way, perform actions in the same order. Like all birds, it fears the unpredictable. Enter and leave the same fields at the same time each day, soothe the hawk from its wildness by a ritual of behavior as invariable as its own. Hood the glare of the eyes, hide the white tremor of the hands, shade the stark reflecting face, assume the stillness of a tree . . . Be alone. Shun the furtive oddity of man . . . Learn to fear. To share fear is the greatest bond of all. The hunter must become the thing he hunts. What is, is now, must have the quivering intensity of an arrow thudding into a tree. Yesterday is dim and monochrome. A week ago, you were not born. Persist, endure, follow, watch.

Hadn't I been trying to coax something out of her? Hadn't I shown up at my desk unfailing, every morning, waiting?

Hadn't I tried to hide the tremor of my hands? Hadn't I let my fears infuse everything I wrote?

"Be alone," "what is, is now," "wear the same clothes": these could be lessons for the artist from the author of "What We Do Not See If We Do Not See" or "On the Perfection Underlying Life" or "The Untroubled Mind." Though Baker's prose is rococo next to Martin's, the passage—with its steering, instructive second person—evokes both reader's guide and transcribed self-talk. (Indeed, as art historian Jaleh Mansoor writes, "The 'you' whom Martin addresses . . . is ostensibly the young artist beset with doubts and anxieties about his or her work.")

A couple years after I left Taos, in the middle of editing this manuscript, I came across an article entitled "You Can Learn to Love Being Alone." Since leaving Taos, I've clicked on a dozen articles like this. I've read books on solitude. Now, to get this revision in shape, I was twelve states away from my husband and my son and Lucy, holed up in a single room. When a writer friend asked how I was doing with my self-imposed residency, I said I hadn't descended into debauchery. "Is that what people do when they're alone?" he asked. In my worst nightmares, that threat still lurked, a patch of black ice I would never see my wheels hit.

This latest article on solitude opens with a majestic photograph of scrubby plains; across the horizon line, against the lilac sky, a Kiger mustang gallops, its black-brown tail streaming behind it. The photos in the piece are big and luscious, perhaps encouraging the reader to pause and meditate, grab a little solitude in plain sight. There are photos of a verdant glen, green trees, a two-pronged path, golden prairie grass. A camper in mist, a redhead's flowing tresses, a trio of horses nuzzle near a wire fence. An elderly man, denim-clad, hands in pockets, in a forest of bare trees. Another man's straddled legs and age-spotted hands clutch three pears, one bitten (silver watchband, no face). A pond reflects a tree on the bank; tented knees by swamp reeds; a hand cupping a white fern; a brick foundation sheltered by amber trees.

The article tells me solitude is calming. Solitude isn't a punishment. Solitude is something to practice. Its value increases as we age. The article suggests bringing a framework to your solitude—journaling, say. Give your solitude a purpose.

My solitude's purpose was Agnes Martin, I think. I'm still getting it wrong. My solitude's purpose was looking inside myself.

If you're lonesome, talk to yourself. Link to 2014 study that finds using second person is self-soothing.

I click the link and skim the study for "second person." I jump to an older study and wonder why I haven't thought about Martin and self-talk: "people refer to themselves as *You* and command themselves as if they are another person in situations requiring conscious self-guidance." Of course, I think. While the essays in *Writings* were often occasioned by Martin speaking at universities or museums—she did so much of that in the seventies, as she was figuring out people weren't left to live all alone—the consistency of her rhetoric, the whittled-down diction, her propensity for the second person, points to a mantric doctrine tailored to the self.

In truth, I clicked on the article hoping it wouldn't mention Agnes Martin. It didn't, so I am relieved. Even though I find the research fascinating and the writing pleasant, I hate articles like this: I scoff at an anecdote of people texting Wordle scores and calling that solitude. But mostly, I hate branding solitude as the latest wellness trend, an antidote for tech overload or societal ills. It's the same reason I scoff when I read about teenage boys documenting their muscle-building on TikTok—even if I've failed, I have tried to make a religion of solitude, of work. Or perhaps, I still resent people who want to be seen. Perhaps I will always have to work through this resentment and envy, the bitterness I feel toward people whose faith in their innate worth assures them others will be receptive to their gifts.

———

From the road we saw a couple walking on a path. The couple may have seen our car on the road. Could they sense our madcap adventurousness? We're leaving soon; anything goes! We took the next turn, parked on an unmarked shoulder, and found a map. The map showed we were on a trail called Bobcat; from here, Lynx, Elk, and Bear knobbed off like vertebrae.

Elk, we decided, a three-mile loop.

The Angel Fire trail network crisscrossed behind big homes with septic tanks in their backyards and a surfeit of tin lawn art. The wind was blowing, noisy and cold. The sky was gray, the clouds coming closer. Lucy bounded through the grass, her tail high and straight.

"I wonder if we're about to be caught in a deluge," my husband said.

He sounded half-joking, and I didn't respond. I still didn't care if we got caught in the rain—secretly I hoped we would get caught in the rain so we would be united in a minor disaster, so we'd have to scoop up Lucy and run.

If I had to run, I still could.

The trail was hard and uneven with gravel. Then the gravel gave way to sand, and the sand became loose dirt, and there was a soft thruway in a grassy field. Wading through the kneecap grass, I wished for a moment that I'd embarked on a novelization, a bastardized fan fiction, "a story of Agnes Martin," where handsome Ag is a character in my plot. (Hand in hand we run the flatlands! The plains of New Mexico, the prairies of Saskatchewan, the cornfields of Illinois!) I didn't know how to put her here, even though her life seemed so alive in my mind.

I looked at my husband. The sun was in his hair, blueing his black curls. He had picked up the dog, and her tail was like a tie slung backward over his shoulder.

I whispered two things to myself:

"Stop fighting happiness."

"Happiness is difficult" (Suzuki).

———

Speaking of epiphanies: The summer before, I was in Detroit writing, and my husband had gone to see his family in

Minnesota. After two years of soberly and drunkenly debating the matter, in our tiny apartment and in our marriage counselor's white-noised, sun-splashed Hollywood office, we were not traveling together because we were at an impasse about the question of children. I was sick with indecision. I'd wept on the phone with a suicide hotline counselor in the Whole Foods parking lot on Santa Monica Boulevard for two hours; I'd given myself an intestinal condition, subsisting on kombucha and salad and mixed nuts; I'd wound up in the ER with a panic attack on top of blood pressure so low, so severe I went into shock. We needed a break.

One night while I was in Detroit, we spoke. The call was tentative and polite. I had very little to report, and my husband told me about a huge cookout with his cousins and backyard games of spike ball or stick ball, whatever ball, a trip to the island and the cabin on the lake, going to the Walker Sculpture Garden and playing rooftop mini golf with our nephews, and maybe the zoo and the butterfly garden and the carousel were part of it. The next day I ran, photographed a blighted church, got grit in my cornea, saw the streets greenlit with God sun, and midstride thought, *Why am I afraid to be happy?* I slowed down. I walked the last block home. I circled the thought like you would with a sculpture and could never do with a painting.

In Detroit, there is a used bookstore inside a former glove factory. There are four dusty floors of books, more than one million books, used and rare, according to the painted bricks on the side of the building. A friend and I went together. He bought me a novel about girls at a performing arts school, who can shift identities when they are beheld by their music teacher; dropped me off at my apartment; and drove back to Ann Arbor. I did not tell him about my epiphany, but the next day, I flew to Minnesota and met my husband and explained: I had been afraid to have a child because I was afraid of becoming a mother, of becoming *my* mother, and yet I was a thirty-four-year-old woman running by herself in a new city—something my mother had never done. I wasn't my mother, and I wouldn't let the fear of becoming her hold me back any longer. Worse than becoming her would be letting fear rule me. Suddenly I saw he was right about what he'd been arguing for months: a child would enrich our lives. When I thought about having a baby, it was terrifying, and thrilling, like everything I loved.

——

Hiking, I was so happy tromping after my husband, seeing the dog's tail, moving through the world, carrying the baby like a prayer. Elk Trail cut into the woods. There were red reflectors stuck to trees, making it clear where you should go next, the way I believed Agnes Martin had trained her intuition or been trained by her intuition (which is not *not* to say guided by schizophrenia). We curved around firs and the forest floor felt springy and good beneath our steps, and pine was on the breeze, and thunder lowed somewhere, and then the trail dipped.

Here was another clearing. And like that there was a gathering of elks.

There were twelve of them, in a formation. They were ash brown, horned, with ears like slippers. Standing in the clearing, they were so still I mistook them for lawn ornaments. An elaborate installation. But no.

My husband spotted them first. We stopped talking and took big soft-shoeing cartoon steps, trying to get close. Closer. Closer. How close could we get?

Then Lucy began to yip at an ungodly pitch and the animals fled, bounding in a herd into the woods. They did not go far. They stood amongst the trees, watching as we passed.

For the remainder of the walk and the meandering ride home, we marveled over the elk. I had never seen the animal in the wild. I had had no sense of how large they were, how stately, how protective of their clan.

That night, I woke up, still dreaming, and saw an elk. A dark shape in a dark mirror after midnight. Half-asleep, I thought: writing about love is like sighting an elk. I heard Martin, too: or trying to represent concretely our most subtle emotions. The animals spook so easily. You can only happen upon them and whisper.

15.

In 1976, Agnes Martin spent three months with a fourteen-year-old boy. The son of hippies living on a New Mexico commune, Peter Mayne was recruited to star in *Gabriel*, what Martin called her art movie. As she told Joan Simon, "I made a movie in protest against commercial movies . . . about deceit and destruction . . . I just wanted to see if people would respond to positive emotions."

That summer, Martin set out to film a visual essay on innocence, beauty, happiness—a movie without misery or negative emotions. In framing the project as an "experiment" to

Simon, three decades after the project's realization, I wonder if she meant an experiment of medium and form or an experiment of intent. Did she make other art in protest?

She hoped to reach a wider audience with *Gabriel*, and so it's ironic that the film is rarely screened. According to a footnote in an essay by Douglas Crimp (then curator at SVA, with whom painter Pat Steir first set off to meet Martin on the mesa), the prints are in bad shape. The colors are compromised, and by all accounts the colors are what Martin cared about.

Martin and Mayne traveling around the Southwest in a big barge of a vehicle, an International Scout II: I find this scenario enchanting. From the beaches of San Sebastopol to snowy Wheeler Peak, Martin yelled, "Okay, action," at Mayne, his cue to walk. Her camera captures long-range shots of walking, close-up shots of walking, point-of-view shots that reveal the vista where he's been walking. Set to Glenn Gould's *Bach: The Goldberg Variations* (and intermittent silence), the film reads more like a sonnet than a story, with a rhyme scheme oscillating between zoom-ins on wildflowers and long-range shots of walking, carrying the boy up and up, from the ocean shores to a mountain peak. In its volta, turning, or returning, to a final image of water.

Sea-summit-sea as I remember, thanks to critic Matthew Jeffrey Abrams. In 2018, Abrams tracked down Mayne and interviewed him in New Mexico. I was surprised and not surprised to learn that, by Mayne's account, Abrams was the first person to seek out the only star (not counting the spectacular landscape) of Martin's only film. *Gabriel* is seen as a fluke or, less kindly, per Abrams, earnest and cringey as a child's skit.

I hadn't seen *Gabriel*. (I still haven't seen *Gabriel*. People who know about Martin, and my project, ask me if I have and then trail off, saying they don't want to bias me.) I've heard the film feels long, nature-clogged (it's seventy-eight minutes). It puts viewers to sleep. Perhaps one senses there was no script. Or that Martin, who bought an editing table for the project, Scotch-taped her own negatives.

I ignore the caveats. First, I know I would probably adore *Gabriel*. Once, at a gallery in Kansas City, I saw a gray-tone video of a Black woman pailing water out of a rowboat, the kind that would've been tethered to a slave ship. Playing in a carpeted room behind a heavy velvet curtain, emitting the rhythmic slosh of waves cresting over the vessel (the piece's only soundtrack), the video lasted thirty-eight or twenty-eight minutes. I stood for its entirety. Around me, other people came and went. Most seemed to have a three-to-five-minute threshold. I treated art films like a low-key endurance sport. I loved the way moving images, unhitched from narrative, stilled me. And I would love *Gabriel*: the Glenn Gould (my husband often played *Bach: The Goldberg Variations*), the locales (my favorite road-trip states), this experiment undertaken by Martin to arouse positive emotion, this neglected offering in her otherwise vaunted catalog: I'd will myself to love it. I'd be all in.

But that was a mistake. That was intellect. Really, I knew *Gabriel* would someday be important to me because it featured a young boy. (In stills, he didn't look fourteen. Maybe nine.) Someday, I would see *Gabriel*, and it would be the film I'd been wanting to see when I was growing my own small baby boy. Someday, I would get what I wanted, and the emotions I'd bridged would pierce through the canopy of aspens or suffuse the acres of sage, and I would remember Martin's summer of protest, and my own.

———

We'd been in New Mexico for two weeks now. We'd leave in three days. I shut my computer and watched the rain. It was early. The rain was light, and a single drop fell through the leaves of a dwarf tree. The drop caused one leaf to bow and spring back; the entire body of the leaf moved, then its tip. The leaves were the color of snow peas and the shape of Brazil nuts. In response to that one bead of water, the whole tree trembled.

It was Monday; the Harwood was closed. To retain concentration, this way of surveilling the world like an intruder, I had to stay at my desk. It was possible. "That you can do it in this moment means you can always do it," Suzuki writes.

I was learning *about* Martin, and in writing about Martin, I attempted to document what I learned *from* Martin—I had to keep that in sight. Because, at times, I was starting to feel like an intruder in her life, breaking in, ransacking the narrative, absconding with all the good stuff and ignoring the hard facts (the way a kid eats the cream out of Oreos, leaving the cookies, spit-sogged, in the tin). I was getting lost in overlapping time and place. A triptych of New Mexico—that pilgrimage to O'Keeffe's Ghost Ranch that I couldn't totally wrap my mind around—the multiplying stints in New York (one color photo of her from 1952, a midnight-blue blouse with the top button undone, an unbuttoned black cardigan, black stud earrings, low ponytail, army-green paint chipping off the wall; these are the Columbia years, and she is seventeen miles from Manhattan at "Last Stop USA," as the military embankment camp Shanks Village was known, which was located in Orangeburg, NY, home to a state psychiatric institution that started performing ECT in the thirties). How important had O'Keeffe been to her? Why was she in Orangeburg? Nothing was simple. When I tried to make it simple, I felt predatory and cruel. Now that I'd read her writing and read writing about her writing, now that I'd sat with her paintings, now that I'd looked at her paintings and looked at reproductions of her paintings, I wasn't sure what good would come of pausing on the breakdown she suffered in 1963, where she was catatonic for nine days, and amnesiac. She wound up in Bellevue, no ID, only a telephone number on a scrap of paper in her pocket. Should I note her psychiatrist, Art Carr, whose fee was paid by Tawney? Other writers liked to report that Agnes watched the seamen's faces clench and grin from her loft on South Street; I wondered if she saw hopscotch lines on the sidewalk, when she began to suspect the square was trouble. Other writers observed that, when she came to New York in 1957, her materials encompassed everything and anything (nails, bottle caps, wood) and how, when she left, that breadth had diminished. Was her leaving New York the moment to focus on, prelude to Portales? Why hadn't I looked up Portales? What was my portal to her? The pregnant sister in Washington State?

Nothing stuck. More and more, the baby occupied my thoughts. The other night, I'd dreamt I found him on his back in a soft flannel swaddle in the middle of a dry golden field. I was crouching over him. Psychologists classify emotions on two axes: valence and intensity. What was the quality of the dream emotion? Its strength? In the field with the baby, I was joyful. The quality was positive, buoyant, fevered, bright. I was joyful to the point of tears glittering my eyes; my face ached from smiling. "Emotions are states of readiness," writes Eric Kandel, "that arise in our brains in response to our surroundings." In the dream, I was ready. I must have been in New Mexico. I had been ready in Albuquerque; I had been ready in Santa Fe. I stroked the baby's cheek and touched his soft, sweet skin. He was flushed. Alert. Warm. I said hello hello hello hello hello hi little boy. I'm your mommy. The word was out before I could resist it. Then I said it again, surprised and delighted by the ease. It was like tasting a food that for your entire life you've hated, only to discover that, not only are beets not horrible, but—raw, shredded, tossed with olive oil and grapefruit juice, salt, on a plate with pink grapefruit supremes and wedges of avocado—beets are wonderful.

In a week, I'd have a tourniquet tied around my upper arm, back in the tower suite at Cedars-Sinai. Beautiful veins, the phlebotomist would say, sea-green veins, survey-says veins, are-you-sure-you-don't-want-to-annihilate-yourself-with-these-veins veins, drawing blood to test for gestational diabetes. I would see my weight. I'd be back in California. Whatever this trip had been would be past, present only in the writing.

———

The more I looked, the more I saw a trace of the maternal in Martin's work. I heard it in her words. It was an immaculate maternal, I thought, free from sex, free from the bodily detritus of pregnancy or childbirth (let alone parenting). The maternal of a perfect teacher. *Perfect*, that staple of Martin's vocabulary, is one definition of *immaculate*, a word that in the Roman Catholic Church denotes freedom from sin— thus, the Virgin Mary conceived of Jesus in the Immaculate Conception, an act trumpeted by none other than the angel Gabriel.

(Thirteen years before she made the film, she painted *Night Sea* ultramarine, a pigment once used exclusively for icons and images of the Madonna.)

Paging an exhibit catalog, I discovered that *Gabriel* was not Martin's first harkening to angels. In 1959, she made a panorama-long work called *The Heavenly Race (Running)*. A graphite line bisects the painting lengthwise (hot-dog fold, in grade school terms). The lower half of the canvas is biscuit white. Squint, and the grain of the canvas appears; the color darkens to the gray of soap scum at the edges; otherwise, it's a solid field. The canvas above the line is occupied by a wing. The wing is composed of three rows of overlapping, rounded-off rectangles in thirty-two columns. In reproduction, the rounded rectangles are the exact size of my pinky, from tip to first knuckle.

Putting my finger over her marks, I understand why I am so quick to see feathers. The shapes resemble the plumage on the hand-traced turkey one makes for Thanksgiving in the earliest art class. Martin taught schoolchildren.

I had read, was reading, would read contradicting ideas about Martin and children: She had not had children in this life. She had not wanted children—she'd already done that, in a past life. No, she had wanted a whole batch of them. Her sister's hard pregnancy. The niece of an early lover said Martin had been good with children. Teaching in Washington, Oregon, New Mexico, Delaware. In the Bronx, she linked grids and trees. She thought children were manifestations of innocence and perfection. "The pretence [sic] of children is not a dream," she writes. "They are playing and they know it."

16.

THAT MORNING, WE DROVE THE Enchanted Circle. It was one of Martin's favorite routes: an eighty-four-mile tour of the National Forest Scenic Byway, ringing 13,161-foot-high Wheeler Peak, snaking ski shanties and wildlife preserves: Taos.org clocks it at four hours. Martin took it fast, eighty miles per hour. The buttermilk leather seats of her white Mercedes would be packed with pals, mouths big and wide and open, belting out show tunes. Forget lingering over the Hondo Valley or a brown trout fish fry; forget Old Westy Red River, Bobcat Pass. I imagine she let the beauty blur.

Already beauty was rushing past us and slipping away as we tooled out of the little Taos downtown and stopped on Route 68 for doughnuts. I was craving a doughnut. I was twenty-seven weeks pregnant. Being pregnant—twenty-seven weeks pregnant!—justified craving: this was craving's time! Being pregnant, also, made craving shameful: my body was expanding enough without an apple fritter the size of a sunflower.

Speaking of shameful, I'd looked up a doughnut shop online when I looked up the Enchanted Circle. We'd been passing a Dunkin' Donuts in town. I wouldn't have needed the internet for that. But I had to have the "best doughnut in Taos." It was stupidly easy to give yourself back to the internet. I hated it. Everything I did on the internet involved consuming or spending money or checking email accounts or online courses that paid me money, which I would then spend on past or present consuming. Even reading *The New York Times*—Martin subscribed—was tainted with my busy hunger: I would itch to pitch an editorial. And in five days, we were leaving. All of that was waiting for me. Time was running out. Twelve weeks until the baby was here, and the semester would begin in a month. I had to make two syllabi and start two grad workshops. I had to write case studies about beer fests and minor league baseball teams for my marketing job. I had to send out writing to magazines when reading periods opened in September. My leave would begin October 1, three days before the C-section. After that, the calendar stopped.

My husband waited in the car with Lucy. The bakery had

a U-shaped glass case, with old-fashioned pastries: salt horns and elephant ears, apple turnovers and cherry strudel squares. The review I'd read said Julia Roberts, aurora borealis of Taos, was a fan of the blue corn cakes.

Not only had I looked up "best doughnut Taos," I had gone to "best doughnut Taos" and spent the last ten dollars from our cash stash, and the doughnuts, plus two piñon coffees, came out to more—seventy-six cents more. At the register, I counted my change. I was thinking: Now I will have to use credit cards. My parents raised me better than this.

The cashier watched. "What are you up to today?"

"We're driving the Enchanted Circle. I'm, uh—"

I'd pretended the pockets in my jean jacket weren't holes. I did not have seventy-six cents.

She took a coin from Give-a-Penny-Take-a-Penny and told me to have a nice day.

In the car, I thought about what Martin says Rothko told her about the distinction between artist and layman: the artist cares about beauty; the layman, money. Stop, I thought.

The sky was the color of dense smoke. The coffee tasted faintly of wood. I put my doughnut on the dashboard and looked at it.

Lucy hopped in my lap.

We passed the D. H. Lawrence Ranch and yellow signs with black silhouettes of cows. We drove into Questa and passed the artist cooperative on the corner. Eight thirty in the morning, the lake was rippled and silver and crowded with fishermen. Then we were twisting and turning, the mountains coming on, and I could feel the road sloping up. The air grew thin.

It was one of those days where I couldn't believe anything had ever been difficult. I was trying to be present and not scribble notes or take photos of billion-year-old feldspar and quartz. I wasn't the driver, so we weren't going fast, and I didn't queue up the soundtrack. My husband played classical radio. I reached into the white paper bag and started picking apart the fritter. Lucy arched her neck like a seal. I gave her a mushy apple.

We kept going up. There were forests on one side and the topographical canvas of the mountain on the other. I felt queasy glancing. I'd gotten sick from the altitude once, back in May, driving through the Rockies, and almost fainted. Chewing helped. I needed to distract myself. I told my husband how Martin drove into her eighties, into her nineties. How she'd take friends from Taos on drives with show tunes singalongs (and haberdashery dress-ups at thrift stores, as Martin's friend Kim Treiber later told me in a Zoom interview). There was earlier evidence the artist wasn't living in total hermitage. Suzanne Hudson notes that *On a Clear Day*, the 1973 series of screen printings that presaged Martin's return to art making, took its title from a mid-1960s Broadway musical, so popular it'd been adapted into a Barbara Streisand vehicle. The story? "A woman who regresses to past lives at the direction of a hypnotist," writes Hudson. "Its title track repeats the memorable lyrics 'On a clear day . . . / You can see forever.'"

My husband remembered seeing *RENT* with his mom.

I got quiet. In this moment I felt like I could see forever, only forever was a dark telescope into a blank mind: death. I'd felt excited and dumb for where I'd steered the conversation about Martin. Excited because this was life beyond the studio, and the more I made of those human details the less (I told myself) I risked reducing Martin to a myth. And yet, my husband had willfully undertaken the experiment in disconnection and minimalism, and quiet art making, with me. Many days, by afternoon I would be exhausted with my text blocks: They were mostly about being pregnant. This one recorded a dream where I'd shaped loaves of bread, that one, a painful conversation with a friend who'd frozen her eggs. The text blocks also captured an unanticipated phenomenon: the more I tried to demythologize Martin, the more I mythologized myself. I felt like a magician, lining up clever mirrors onto certain qualities of her personhood—self-sufficiency, a reticence about sexuality, her relationship to beauty, her renouncement of material pursuits—that would reflect the qualities most damning in me. So, I was romanticizing myself, making myself her foil. To use a poetic heuristic, you're a Dickinson or a Whitman. She was Dickinson; I was Whitman, I thought, a body barreling through dense, ribald forests of language. When I got too claustrophobic in paragraphs, I stopped making sense. Then, I'd get up to read on the patio or read in the hammock, and on my way outside, I'd see the bedroom door cracked open, my husband on the loveseat writing an afternoon poem, the thirty-fifth or thirty-sixth draft of a poem. He'd read me a draft the other night; the clarity of his lines reminded me of how Martin's canvases absorbed and radiated light. Now I was telling him about her joyriding. Was I destroying Martin's cred?

The classical music started to crackle; I was still eating the doughnut. One hand roaming around in the white bag, fingers sticky with apple goo. I'd plumbed the fritter's center. I was chipping off the white-hard glaze from its knobby edges. Tear, nibble, share with Lucy, wipe fingers on grubby napkin bent like kindergarten origami.

Now I felt so horrible I could only take small sips of air. I had just remembered how bad it had been in Colorado. It was worse here. I was light-headed and nauseated. No morning sickness this bad. I had worried I would suffocate, or the baby would suffocate. I picked up my phone and searched "pregnant altitude baby damage." I had no service.

My husband asked if I wanted to pull over. I put my face on my knees and said keep going. I was remembering being in other cars, eating snacks on car trips as a child, and instead of thinking about Martin, and her singing drives, or the road-bound lessons she'd imparted to Peter Mayne, I was remembering sucking the salt off pretzel rods when I was thirteen. I remembered that more precisely than anything I had ever learned. And I was happy, so happy, to think how my son might look back on a big doughnut in a white bag, belting bodacious showtunes, traveling on numbered highways, through towns he'd forget, that I forgot I was suffocating.

————

Dark thunder dawned across Camino del Medio. The dwarf pines, with their bilious orange trunks, shed russet needles. In the last hour, the temperature had dropped twenty degrees; tomorrow it would storm. At ten after four, my friend called.

"HiJoAnnaHowAreYou?" she said.

It was her usual greeting: bum-rush-interrogation laced with skepticism. Her tone was dubious. Now I'd try so hard to be calm and affable, even as the lonely self-pity set in, I wouldn't tell her anything.

"Good," I hurried, "how are you?"

My friend gushed. She led euphoric, transitioned into critical. She told me about her newish new boyfriend, how in love they were, how they were having so much sex, where they were having so much sex, the ways in which the so much sex was so good, also how her sister was being cruel about her boyfriend's station in life (bartender) and cruel about everything. I found her behavior—soaring away from stable adult life on the winds of base lust—at once admirable and sad.

"She says I'm lucky to be an aunt. That I don't do the work of kids, I can just leave them. It's like she's saying, 'It's okay, you'll never have kids.'"

I didn't follow that final leap, and I sort of saw Cruel Sister's point, but asking my friend was useless. She would tell me I didn't understand babysitting nephews, I didn't know what it was like being judged for being unmarried, babyless. This was partially my friend's personality, and partially my own self-consciousness, ready to feel judged or blamed for my very existence.

My friend had always wanted children. Not in an infant-crazed fervor, but calmly, rationally. Even when she was depressed. Her desire for children, that vote for futurity, persisted, a sure, solid hope. This had long reassured me I would never change my mind.

I asked my friend about her new job (genius teammates!), her new boss (quirky polos!), her camping (North Carolina!). She didn't ask, so I didn't offer anything about Martin. Or the Harwood. Or what I was writing, how I was writing (would I have had my wits about me to church up the text boxes, call them "prose blocks"?). Or trying to be disconnected for a few weeks. Or books, though we usually talked books: no shouting out Nancy Princenthal's bio or the *Writings* I toted around like a missalette. No describing Taos, the neighborhood, the casita, leagues of pale-gold sand, how the sky was an object lesson in being nothing, how the prairie dogs played in the front yard of the hospital. Unless we were united in a cause—being accountability buddies in our dieting, laughing at the same stand-up set—our dynamic was one where my friend assumed the big sister role and I complied, a dynamic that suited me well: I was in subservience to all my female friends.

"Anyway," my friend said, forty minutes in. "How are you feeling, being pregnant?"

I was on Plaza Cañon Drive, following the cloverleaf roundabout. I paused. I had a sororal/stoic "pretty good!" queued up. But pretty good wasn't real. I wished I had memorized something from *Writings*—maybe, an experiment within this experiment, I could deadpan-recite a Martin text. A generality wouldn't cut it. Maybe the ultimate test of erasing my ego would be to recuse myself from conversation. But that's not what I wanted. I wanted to say, I'm good but I'm trying to walk this line of not caring about gaining weight and also acknowledge it's uncomfortable gaining weight without going crazy; I'm thinking about it and I'm trying not to think about it. Wouldn't she understand? Our friendship stemmed from anorexia, mine and hers, a slow, sloshing year of shyly eyeing each other's collarbones, mainlining Fiona Apple lyrics like Sweet'N Low. We'd sustained a decades-long dialogue about weight, working out, restricting, purging, being okay with food, the brief rush of being unokay with food. Whether we were on the phone cross-country or taking a walk on the High Line, there was always a point where one of us asked, tiptoeingly, "How's food stuff?"

Across the street, the parking lot of Gutters was packed. My husband and I joked about going bowling, forgetting I'd have to roll the ball between my legs. No one had the money. Also, paying to waste your time? I cinched my LA cap.

"Pretty good," I said, finally.

"Yeah?"

"Sorry, it's loud and windy here," I looked down. Brown beer bottle glass glittered in the dirt. "The baby's kicking a lot, which is actually really cool."

"Wow . . . That's great."

I didn't know what to say. I thought, *Maybe she wants more.* Maybe she wants to be the person to make me say the thing I'm scared to say. Or maybe what I had to say was changing.

"I didn't bring my scale, though. So that's weird. It's weird—not knowing."

There was a pause. "JoAnna, I'm—why would you be weighing yourself?"

"I always do," I said. This was true. "It keeps me honest."

"JoAnna, that's really sad. You're growing a human life. Do you know what that means? That's a big fucking deal—that's the most important thing you can do. You shouldn't be thinking about weighing yourself at all. Not even—I mean, I'm sorry. I feel sorry for you. I'm sorry you can't relax and be a person, and I'm sorry you can't enjoy this time."

"I am enjoying this time," I said, and that was true, too. "It's not like weighing myself even affects me anymore. I eat whatever I want to eat. I mean, I want ice cream every day and I don't eat that—but that's not exclusive to being pregnant."

"You're building a house for your baby. Why is weight even a factor?"

"It isn't. I just like to know. It's like seeing the address on the house."

We had an understanding, an unspoken contract: even if we were no longer anorexic, thinness was still a life-organizing concern. She couldn't expect pregnancy to possibly expunge all that—so why was she foisting that expectation on me? I felt wildly estranged from her and so sad about what this augured for our friendship.

"You know no matter how much weight you gain, JoAnna, you'll still be the same person." My friend used her dad voice. "What you weigh doesn't affect who you are at all."

I was silent.

"I hope you have ice cream every goddamn day if you want to. You're pregnant."

She was jealous, I thought; jealousy made her moralizing. Perhaps she thought it was unfair that I was pregnant, after I'd spent two decades staunchly against children. That whole time, she had wanted a baby. Perhaps it irritated her that I was still desperate to transcend my human body when I was completing arguably the single most transcendent biological process possible (save death). Perhaps she was afraid that she would never be pregnant; perhaps she was sure she would. Perhaps on a clear day, a hypnotist had told her a baby was in her future. Perhaps she wanted to live through me. Perhaps she was tired of us pursuing thinness in tandem; perhaps she felt competitive; perhaps she needed to stop seeing us as kindred spirits. Or perhaps, without me uttering a single word about Martin's incandescent pink bars or lush desert environs, she knew my obsession with this world of vast, distilled beauty was born of immoderate terror—a glorified invisibility stunt: if I'm going to be erased by motherhood, let me control my own erasure—apex of anorexic thinking—like Martin.

"Hey, I'm just getting home," I said. "I should get to work."

"Really?" The doubtful tone was back. "I thought you were taking time off work."

I couldn't hold back any longer. "Writing work," I said. "I'm here writing about Agnes Martin."

———

That evening, we took Lucy to Baskin-Robbins. My husband got a scoop of vanilla for her. I got a kid's cookies 'n' cream cone. I thought about texting my friend.

Afterward, at the park, we saw a pair of older women walking around the peewee football field. One of them called out to us.

"Beautiful—" she said, expression soft, like a thumbprint in dough.

"Thank you!"

She wasn't finished. "You have a beautiful belly!"

I blinked, surprised, happy. Anticipating a compliment for Lucy, I'd accepted it, easily, without hesitation.

17.

THAT MORNING, I'D TRIED writing about schizophrenia. I had read about schizophrenia and taken many pages of notes, sketching the hemispheres of the brain. But when I looked at those pages and thought about how to translate them into my six-inch squares, they made me nervous. I didn't want to get Martin wrong. I didn't want to harm her by overemphasizing or disregarding her mental illness, transforming her into a pathology. Or an eccentric. Or a mystic—she blatantly objected to that: "No you're not a mystic when you respond to beauty." She was a person. As smitten as I was with her biography, I didn't want to link the issues of *the disordered mind*—the title of the book I'd been reading—with her art. I could hear all too well the cause-and-effect plot my students would force onto her paintings: She paints peaceful, pretty lines because she's tortured by inner demons. Her art lets her control what she can't in her head. The grid is, like, her way of bringing order to her life. "What does it mean?" my students asked of poems, demanding everything from metaphors to enjambments to ampersands have an articulable rationale. If life were something to be assigned, analyzed, and solved in this manner, I would rather have endless notes on schizophrenia. Make of them what you will:

> Executive function, dementia praecox
> Three million people in the US, 1 percent of the
>   population nationwide
> Jack Kerouac Brian Wilson John Nash
> thorazine clozapine risperidone olanzapine
> tremors rigidity bending forward
> dopaminergic pathways: mesolimbic (thought, mean-
>   ing, emotion: excessive dopamine receptors) and
>   nigrostriatal (spatial, motor: deficient dopamine)
> dilation of lateral ventricles—hollow spaces carrying
>   cerebrospinal fluid
> thinning of gray matter

The brain was an organ and a canvas. Neuropsychology made it a paint-by-number: certain colors applied to certain regions would change temperament.

As much as I wanted notes to be sufficient, I didn't know how to provide a convincing alternative to the very reading I was so desperate to stave off. As I imagined the baby's development, which I thought, for someone pregnant with her first kid, I was doing a fairly good job being cool about, schizophrenia scared me. Unlike depression or other mood disorders, schizophrenia is rooted in anatomical defects. In *The Disordered Mind*, Kandel writes:

> During pregnancy, environmental factors, such as nutritional defects, infections or exposures to **stress** or toxins, may interact with genes to increase the risk that the fetus will develop abnormally functioning dopaminergic pathways. Malfunctioning pathways set the stage for developing schizophrenia years later, when the brain of the adolescent responds to the stress of everyday life by generating excessive dopamine.

I was terrified. What if, in some cruel irony, the pressure I'd put on myself to learn from Martin and live like Martin were harming the baby, corrupting his dopaminergic pathways? It would be my fault. My pride. My egotistical desire to be a better writer. My inability to be happy with the gift. The baby. If my ambitions hurt him, I would hate myself forever. The thoughts made me want to die. I felt panicky, listless.

I took my phone up to the top bunk. The gold and turquoise comforter was smoothed out, the pillows plump. A couple times, I'd brought *Zen Mind, Beginner's Mind* up here and read on my side, a sham wedged between my knees. You sleep with your back to the world when you're pregnant—you have to—no lying on your back allowed.

I turned on my phone. I had broken that rule many times; rules were fiction—did it matter if I watched porn? I lowered the volume; I didn't lower the shades. If the property manager came into the backyard, or my husband, they would see a woman looking at a small screen.

I put on a long video, nearly an hour. Here, a sex shop and a woman who worked there. There was a back room, a chamber of tortures. The woman had dirty-blond hair and a tired neck. Her eyes were undressing the customer who came in to undress her. Stripped, belly down, her hips hinged over the edge of the counter. One man shoved his cock in her mouth. Another man spat on her asshole and began fucking her there. I felt a loose trembling in my thighs. Like if I weren't lying down I might collapse. The woman's lipstick was smeared now, an abrasion over her mouth. Her eye makeup was running; there were specks of black set in the foundation. A girl crouched against the counter, holding a vibrator to the woman's pubic mound. One cock out, a thicker cock in. Close-up on a comma of mascara.

After two minutes, I shut off my phone, aroused and furious. What was I doing? Why this incessant need to watch a woman endure endless violation and call it pleasure? I felt revealed: the pornography made it so obvious: I identified with the victim—I fetishized that position. Pain was the price you paid for pleasure. That didn't make me strong. I was too weak to feel good.

How much confusion would I tolerate?

I shoved the phone under a pillow and carefully stepped down the ladder. I sat in the black leather chair. The caster scratched the floor. My fingers were cold shaking over the keyboard.

———

"What are you thinking?" I asked my husband.

He considered the ground, middle distance. "I'm looking at the flowers and the plants," he said. "Those big dandelions. I know they're probably not dandelions."

At Juniper Road, we turned home. The rain was forecasted to return, and we were prepared to get wet—I wanted to get wet. The casita was close and warm.

"It feels like the baby's down here," I said, rubbing the podgy bulge at my pelvis, the way I used to rub my hip bones. I pictured the baby on a ledge inside my body, resting his chin on his forearm, ponderous and peaceful like my husband.

"Are you excited for the newest member of our family?"

"What day is it? Almost two and a half months . . ."

We passed an empty corner lot, a northern New Mexico prairie. The grasses were tall and long shafted. They were golden and brown and yellow and barely green. There were coyotes in this neighborhood, I'd read. They could be lurking in the grasses now, bellying down, yapping at the dirt, chomping field mice and prairie dogs. It struck me how

utterly fearless Agnes Martin must have been, to live alone
in the wilderness for years. I thought about our clean, well-
lighted casita, the whirlpool tub my husband would soak
in after a walk, the enormous back-bedroom windows, the
landscaped firepit. I could not have dug the firepit myself,
pregnant or not—nor did I want to. No matter how much
I searched for similarities—the mother, the childhood supe-
riority, the swimming, the indefatigability in all manner of
work, the exultation of work, the repetitive things we did
with our hands: one summer in high school, I worked in a
snack bar at the pool and passed fifty minutes between adult
swim breaks by drawing on pieces of scrap paper right triangles filled with obsessively straight lines—no matter how
much I wanted my state of mind to be analogous to Martin's,
it wasn't. I felt pathetic, considering these resemblances. She
was a dead, brilliant, millionaire who channeled unworldly
beauty. I was in fumbling pursuit.

   And this, it hit me, was nothing new: I had been seeking transcendence outside myself for decades. What if such
extravagant pursuit of Martin's ethos would simply keep me
impoverished from my own? I was pursuing her to distract
myself from what pursued, what pursues all of us: an end
where our life's pursuits—painting, writing, walking, running, driving white cars and black cars, borrowing kids, having kids—finally halt. A shiver ran through me. I scanned
the ocherous grass. Did coyotes attack people? Was I a person
with the baby inside me? Was I more of an animal? I walked
faster.

"I guess I'm—no, I'm excited about the baby," I said. "Are you?"

My husband sounded solemn. "I am." Admitting it seemed to release a pressure valve. "After all this buildup, I'm just ready to have this third *person* . . . hanging out with us. Being his own little person. Doing the things people do. Seeing the world. I'll be ready when he's here, and for now, I'm glad we have this time. This time to be us. This babymoon."

"It's not a babymoon," I said, sharply. "I didn't mean for it to be a babymoon."

"No, I know. It's that. That and other things. A babymoon, research. Writing time."

Writing time: saying it like that, writing sounded portioned, compartmentalized, the spot for a sippy cup on a high chair tray. Writing time, play time, snack time: infantilizing. Recently, I discovered in one of my books a photograph of Martin taken by Diane Arbus. Martin's seated in her South Street studio; it's a year before she leaves New York. She's wearing her standard quilted boilersuit, a garment so utilitarian it transformed all her time into working time. Only, that was wrong. I was reading the photograph as an endless present, when she must've taken the boilersuit off, donned the long trench coat and a hat, walking shoes—I'd seen her in Keds-like walking shoes—not the pigeon-toed loafers she wore in this shot. One Friday in February, several years later, Ann Wilson would tell me over the phone about marketing with Martin, buying potatoes and milk. I knew her life had been more than painting and gallery shows and mental breakdowns: there had been tugboat rides and ferry rides, beach-hopping in New Jersey, camping upstate—and yet I still wanted to believe Martin's time had *mostly* been spent painting. Or, if not painting, better spent than mine. That was what my friend had been saying—worrying about food was a waste of my time. Some part of me knew that, too, recognized the way sustaining even a low-grade dislike of my body kept me fluent in self-hatred; I thought of the notes I wrote in my journal between text blocks—*one more, you can do this, you've got this.* When I went to inpatient treatment, my senior year of college, I attended an occupational therapy session where we wrote letters to our bodies fifteen years in the future. Before we started writing, a counselor reminded us that changing our self-talk was critical to recovery. "Think about what you say to yourself," the counselor had said. "Would you talk to your best friend or your sister like that?" I wouldn't, I didn't, and yet I acted like I was the exception—I could handle the tough self-talk. I could handle seeing my weight, "keeping it real." But I had grown up with a mother who constantly belittled herself. If I didn't rein this in now, my baby would see the same self-hatred in me.

I couldn't let that happen.

In front of us, a driveway festooned with Tibetan prayer flags. The Virgin of Guadalupe whispered *demur* from an address plate. I bit the inside of my cheek. We were leaving in two days. I could not compare us forever.

"It has been incredible writing time," I said. "Thank you for making this an adventure. We're going to think back on this one day. We're going to tell the baby." I paused. "I don't know other people who do this."

———

All afternoon, I was on the lookout for a sign. In 2002, the year Martin turned ninety, the mayor of Taos decreed Agnes Martin Week! There was an international conference. Champagne and cake. Banners. The kind of sign I was after was loud and flapping in the wind, telling me how to do what I was supposed to be doing.

That night, my husband told me he'd planned a date. After dinner, he said, get in the car.

"What is one quintessential Taos experience we haven't had . . . yet?" He was driving slower than his usual slow, ceremoniously.

"Just tell me."

"We're going to Dennis Hopper's grave."

My heart sank. I'd hoped he was taking me to a hidden Martin site. Maybe he'd learned which toy shop housed her last studio (Twirl, I'd later discover, from Martin's pal Kim Treiber). Maybe he'd befriended the director of the Harwood or the owner of the Trading Post Café (where Martin liked steak, sliced tomatoes, and Chianti for lunch). Maybe he'd bribed the chummy guard to tell him beneath which apricot tree she was buried.

Those expectations were ludicrous. Visiting Dennis Hopper's grave made sense. My husband was interested in Hopper because of his role in *Blue Velvet*. I can't remember what he read first: that Hopper had lived in Taos, or that part of *Easy Rider* had been filmed in Taos, but either way, several nights ago, we'd watched the movie on his laptop, and it had made me nostalgic for a circle of punk-and-classic-rock-loving art students I'd hung out with in high school, half a semester when I almost forgot I had an eating disorder, I was so happy listening to the Ramones or the Who, painting and smoking cigarettes; it had made me think about riding on the back of my father's motorcycle, through cornfields, how blissfully simple it was being on the road, and I'd written a text block about wanting to be an easy rider, by which I meant I wanted to channel a say-yes-to-adventure-and-let-me-contain-multitudes, heart-in-my-throat spirit in my life, and by my life I meant not just these last days in Taos (though we did have a plan for our last full day to go to the swimming hole at Manby Hot Springs, where Hopper and Peter Fonda and their commune-robed girlfriends frolic and splash and play sea monster while The Byrds' upbeat strummer "Wasn't Born to Follow" plays), but life with the baby—I wanted to be as impish and swarthy as Hopper, as long-limbed and gamine as the hippie girls. While my son was growing up, I wanted him to know the ambling loveliness of a river current ruching like silk around him while he paddled naked and free.

We drove past the Chow Cart and the Sagebrush Inn, and soon turned toward Mora. We'd driven through Mora. In Mora, the courthouse was a mobile home, the only business in business an Allsup's gas station that sold deep-fried slices of pepperoni pizza.

"Where are we?" I said.

"Rancho de Taos."

Earlier, he'd explained to me what ranchos were. The road was empty. It arrowed straight toward the mountains.

From Espinoza, we rumbled down a side street that cut into nothingness and turned into unmarked Jesus Nazareno Cemetery. We parked in chalky gravel.

We got out of the car. I had friends who had sex in graveyards, but this one didn't feel sexy or mysterious or romantic. We were out here alone. It was a forgotten, sad, out-of-the-way place where a carnival might post up. It was raining.

My husband was looking at his phone.

"It's supposed to be right here," he said, motioning.

I looked around at the color photos stuck on the tombstones. Carnations lavished the crosses, guarded by lawn gnomes.

My husband brought up a video on his phone. A point-of-view shot: the camera tracked to Hopper's grave.

"It should be right here," he said, pointing at a mound labeled *Garcia*.

"Maybe he was really Garcia?"

We shuffled on the soft damp gravel. In the distance: boxcars, the paint worn off in jags; wire fence necklacing a chokecherry tree. And then, here: maybe two hundred plots.

"J," my husband called. "This is it."

He was standing, aiming the flashlight on his phone at a large wooden cross. Hopper's visage was carved into the interstice. This was long-haired Hopper, small mouth, rectilinear nose. Bandanas wrapped the cross: faded pink, motor-oil black, paisley, chili peppered, elephant print. An American flag fluffed like a jabot. The whole monument was wrapped in silver ball bearings and Mardi Gras beads and a leather lariat.

For a while I lost myself in the druggy harum-scarum of these tributes, the quail feathers and peacock quills and baseball hats and wildflowers. Though I felt little about Hopper, I was moved—even calmed—by the tender, messy beauty of his grave.

Looking at the plot strewn with fir cuttings and baby's breath, my thoughts went to my own death. I didn't want to die when I didn't want to die; I didn't want to think about dying even when I did want to die. But when I did think about dying, I thought about, first, my absolute terror at the cessation of consciousness, and then, second, how many people I loved would remain after I was gone. When I imagined death, there was a small funeral, the full cast of my life in attendance. My husband, my parents, my siblings, my friends, maybe an old teacher—and my son. And yet, once my son was born, I would begin fearing for my own life like never before. I didn't want him to grow up without me. I didn't want to miss anything.

I felt a swell of tenderness, looking at the offerings from Hopper's fans: mortar and pestle, two Mary prayer cards, five toy motorcycles, terra-cotta rosettes, a bottle of bourbon, and a rolled-up scroll in a velvet pouch. My husband and I stood side by side. He squeezed my hand.

Perhaps I'd been all wrong about Martin leaving New

York. Perhaps, even though *Easy Rider* came out in 1969, when she'd already rented the land on Portales mesa, perhaps the film's spirit was alive in her, too. Perhaps her eighteen-month road trip had not meant the death of her art career but a rebirth, the adoption of a roving, simpler self. Perhaps she was renouncing pain, pain as a trope of the brilliant, tormented artist vying for fame and recognition in the cruel city—a role that no longer fit.

18.

THE DRAPES WERE OPEN, THE shades up in the back bedroom. Out in the yard, green things, weed things, sour yellow grasses, wild daisies clamoring.

I stepped outside with my coffee. In front of the rickety wooden folding chair-and-table setup on the paver bricks outside the casita, sweet ants had built a series of site-specific powdery dirt volcanos. I heard a clang: a Brillo-bearded Texan staying in the next casita recycled more Monster. In my notes, I wrote, "You say, 'what can I do,' and then you wait."

What was I waiting for? I would pack up and leave tomorrow.

My husband came out with a book. He sat down on the porch. The wind was listening. The air smelled like dry gravel and old sun. We were waiting for 1:00 p.m., when the temperature would be in the mid-nineties, so we could go swimming. Only I'd tried on my swimsuit for the first time in two months, and I was on a tirade.

"I don't even know if we should go," I said. "I look disgusting."

"Why would you say that?" my husband said. He had put his book down. "You're just trying to engage in conflict."

"You're right," I said. "What else am I good for? I'm garbage. I'm expendable. You and your mother could raise the baby; you'd be happier that way. Try it." My voice flattened like a worm. "Imagine me gone from this chair."

I did not say I wanted to kill myself. I did not say I wanted to disappear or be blinked out from life. Here was a new desire, and a new desire constituted progress: I wanted to be alone.

If I were alone, I wouldn't dramatize my discontent or exploit the patience of another person. Your feelings are not reality, my therapist often said. They're weather. Who would get worked up about the weather?

Alone I would step into unfeeling, a temperature-less silence.

I blithered some of this. My husband got up.

"When you're ready to be decent and come inside, maybe

we can have lunch and go for a swim. I want to do that with you, JoAnna."

Lucy scurried into the casita with him.

I shut my eyes. *You're getting worse*, I thought. Even though Martin said there was "no such thing as going backward in anything," I didn't believe her.

———

Behold: Taste bud for weeks, skin pinking, eyelids, nostrils, fingernails, hiccups. The third trimester begins at twenty-eight weeks. (Shaky gestational math.)

A thesaurus of symptoms: fatigue, exhaustion, lethargy, ennui, restless legs, insomnia. Tingling palms, tingling phalanges, tingling cortices.

A teacher who repeated *Stanza means room*.

A stanza of life: *matrescence*: the period of becoming a mother.

A nausea of bad jokes: "Ouch! You've got a kicker! Get ready, soccer mom!"

A woman from Canada, who began menstruating at sixteen, was called *slut*, calls sex the same process over and over, a destruction, a rage, entering the third trimester of her life.

The artist cracks open the final nesting doll: one painted peg of wood, alone at last.

Behold: tactility, emergency, endless omissions.

Behold: In the third trimester, dendritic spines begin to form. Dendritic spines enable working memory. They develop in pyramidal neurons in the prefrontal cortex. All dendritic spines undergo pruning, but in schizophrenics the pruning goes berserk.

Behold: The artist must *live very carefully*. The artist becomes a mother to her work or a mother to her womb's work, so behold, "Beauty is in the eye of the beholder" is not about seeing but possession and ownership, grabbing. Rather than a glimpse, a grasp.

———

After a few minutes, I knew my husband wasn't coming back. I listened with my ear next to the screen door. When I heard the shower start, I got up and walked as fast as I could away from the casita.

I didn't bring water. Or my phone. The baby was fat. His bones were solidifying this week. He would be fine. There was the neuron thing. The baby might even be able to detect a light shone through my stomach, a candling for my chick.

Soon I was off the property, turning right and turning right again, and the sun was blazing down. The leached yellow sand extended in every direction. The mountains loomed like gray waves. I must have been moving because I heard the cacophony of wind, plants and rocks and invisible animals skittering, and the foghorn of my brain.

Padding on the calico-soft ground in the hottest hour of the day, I was feeling horrible, dizzy and weak. I was not doing well. It hurt to focus. Tiny white moths playing in the sagebrush flitted in slow motion. I closed my eyes—it was painful and hard. I needed to turn around. Only I didn't know if it would be quicker to loop around the block or re-trace my steps. I bent over, sniffed the dirt and sun baked into my knees, and raked my fingers in the sand on the shoulder. It was hot. If I stayed upside down long enough, I would tip. I pictured the baby curling up inside me, making himself small and still. Finding what comfort he could on the uterine pavilion. I could learn from him. I could lie down in the gravel, in the wildflowers. Let the sun shine through me. I could firm up or move out of my life.

I righted myself, dizzy. I was seeing neon bars of light. "Dammit, dammit, dammit," I whispered. "Just get home, just get back to the casita, you've got this."

A shiver ran through me and I shook like Lucy when she was out of the bath, before she began racing around our apartment like a whirling dervish, trying to find her scent. I started jogging. My breath was thick in my throat.

Go on, do it, I thought. If I exercised, maybe my head would clear up. I ran a few yards. My body was so heavy. The sun was so hot. I had to walk. I ran again. I stopped. I ran again. Finally, I was back at the casita.

The bedroom door was closed. I heard the tower fan. The casita's smallness, the piddly square footage of our plan, was heartbreaking. I didn't want the baby to be isolated from our friends and family—why was I trying to cultivate an aptitude for that? I didn't want him to see his parents in a bad marriage. And now my husband was working. I had exhausted him and driven him away. I remembered why I had been so excited to go to Manby Springs: I had decided to believe that it was a swimming hole that Agnes Martin could've loved. This was confabulation, but I had tried to research where she swam, which municipal pool it was that she donated, and gotten nowhere.

I went into the bathroom. A little sun came in through the window over the shower; I kept the row of bulbs over the vanity off. Very dim and deep blue. All the travel toiletries were gone from the counter. We'd used everything. Look at us, I thought. I drank cold water from the tap.

I would tell my husband I was sorry and salvage the day.

I lifted my shirt. My breasts had gotten dense. My stomach was like that, too, a drum. Pregnancy had made my body possessed and hard.

I was sitting on the toilet, peeing, pleased with my decision to humble myself in apology, when the stream of urination was cut off by a slithering, heavy plop.

My heart lurched.

I wiped. The paper was bloody.

With my shorts around my thighs, I waddled over to the light.

There was a spherical mass in the toilet, a clot the size of a plum. Dark blood, with a hood of milky greenish yellow around it. The tissue looked soft and spongiform, a microscoping of a virus. For a second I worried it was the baby. Then I remembered the 3D ultrasound, the articulated fingers and toes, the snub nose that had been sketched out more than a month ago. This was like a piece of raw meat vomited before stomach acid could break it down.

Shaking, I flushed the toilet, washed my hands, and splashed cold water on my face. I stepped out into the casita and saw my reflection in the mirror behind the wood stove. I did not look like a substantial person. I looked very, very lost.

I thought, if I have hurt the baby, my husband will never forgive me.

I found my phone on the bookshelf. There wasn't a single pregnancy guide. I hated all the Martin books. How could she help me? I *was* a mother now. And I'd been so ungrateful for that gift—of being this baby's mother—that I might've horribly, horribly fucked it up. I turned on my phone and went into the side yard. I could barely breathe.

I stood by the hammock, facing away from the house, listening to the rings.

Finally, my mother picked up.

"Something's wrong," I said.

"Are you okay? Is—"

I shook my head. She couldn't see me. What had I done?

"Everyone's fine," I said. "I'm . . . I mean, I'm fine. I don't know if the baby is fine. I was out on a walk, and it was really hot and I wasn't feeling well, and when I came back I used the toilet and—this is gross, I shouldn't be telling you this."

"You should be telling me this," she said. "I'm your mother. That's what I'm here for."

"I peed and there was blood. A lot of blood. Like . . . a hard mass of blood. What if I hurt the baby?"

I couldn't stop crying. I wound my fingers through the hammock ropes and squeezed. I wanted to rip it out of the tree. I wanted to rip down the whole tree. What had I done?

"Calm down, JoAnna," she said, "calm down. Sweetie, JoAnna. Sweetheart. Take a deep breath. It sounds like it might be your mucus plug. Can you google that?"

"A mucus plug?" I said, revolted.

"I lost mine right before I had you. It just came out when I was giving a urine sample in the doctor's office. Can you google it?"

I did not say I'd turned off the Wi-Fi on my computer. "Would you stay on the phone with me?" I said.

"I'll stay on the phone with you as long as you want. What else am I doing?"

"Talking to me," I said, sheepishly.

"That's right. I'm talking to my firstborn daughter, pregnant with my first grandson. And she's about to go back to LA. Are you excited?"

"Yeah," I said. I was. "Okay, I'm about to google. I'm so scared."

"Don't be scared."

I groaned and gagged, scrolling through the images.

"Is that how yours looks?" my mother asked.

"I don't know," I whined. I couldn't tell if I was overdramatic or finally appropriately concerned. I couldn't believe I'd flushed the toilet. If I hadn't had my phone off in the other room, if I'd been scrolling through news or email, I would've had a phone in hand to document this evidence.

"Call your OB," she said. "See what they say."

They said maybe it was the mucus plug, and to go to the hospital immediately: that's when I told my husband that I would be driving to Holy Cross.

"This is how you want to spend your last day in Taos?" he said.

"My doctor said to."

"Because you called your doctor," my husband said.

"Don't you get it?" I was rushing around, packing a tote bag with my notebook and the biography and spare underwear and socks, wondering if this meant the baby was coming. "This could be a sign that I'm about to go into labor. It was for my mom."

"Why did she tell you that?" he said.

"Because I asked her!" I said, getting angry. "I asked her for help. And she listened. She did help."

"She encouraged you to go to the emergency room?"

"No! She told me to call my doctor. She helped, okay? Back down! If it's a problem, I can drive myself."

"You're not driving yourself to the hospital, JoAnna," my husband said. "Don't be ridiculous."

I'd walked past Holy Cross four or five times in the last two and a half weeks. Walking, getting to the prairie dogs in the hospital yard seemed to take forever; now, it was three minutes in the car until he dropped me off at the ER.

There was one other person in the waiting room. Because I was pregnant, said the triage nurse, I would be taken to a bed right away.

My husband apologized—he seemed surprised at how quickly I was given a hospital gown and fitted with a pink elastic strap across my belly to monitor contractions.

———

While I was lying in the hospital bed, I thought about how, in the middle of the night, I'd woken up muttering the phrase *mute black painting*. Yesterday I had gone to the Harwood and written down the phrase: *a cloud in the sky of the museum*.

That was what it was like to look at *Tundra*.

I'd sat on a bench, crackled leather, the color of chocolate milk. Upstairs was nothing like downstairs. On the second floor of the Harwood, directly above the Martin Gallery, there were four or five rooms, display cases, video installations, a small show of work made by a girl art prodigy from New Mexico who had died tragically young, and *Tundra*, the last painting Martin made before leaving New York.

Looking at the balking, bleak *Tundra* ("a mature grid," I'd read), I felt a dull hungry melancholy. The paintings in the gallery had given me a sense of lightness and hope. *Tundra*, on the other hand, made me hate myself. The butterscotch leather tote bag at my feet. My Chanel espadrilles and my Chanel sunglasses. My wedding ring, my engagement ring. Could I uneat everything I had eaten? Stupid shiny foil protein bar wrappers.

The painting was so empty. Mature, in *Tundra*, meant larger. The cells were spacious and somehow dark, even though the acrylic was off-white or warm pale gray. Etiolated,

I wanted to say. No. The color of blanched newsprint. Here Martin had drawn fewer discrete marks. A little graphite— two vertical lines, one horizontal line—cordoned off six rectangular panes on the canvas. Also in 1967, she painted *Adventure*. Same size, pretty much same cement shade: That painting consists of seventeen equidistant horizontal lines. The lines reach to the edge of the canvas, a magnified sheet of college-ruled loose-leaf.

Taken together, the pair suggest an arctic exploration—a mission on which the old artist will freeze herself to death? The grays, after all, gave way to what one critic called Martin's period of famine. The six years where she didn't paint or draw. Where she drove and wrote and built. It wasn't until 1973, when she traveled to Germany and London, and made the screen prints comprising *On a Clear Day*, that Martin began making art again. Did it feel like a return or a new beginning? Is there a difference?

Even knowing that *Tundra* was not quite the midpoint of her life, that the luminous pinks I'd first crushed on came later, that *Gabriel* came later, that the majority of her output came later, I still felt a rise of sadness in my throat. I got up and went downstairs.

I wandered into the Agnes Martin Gallery one last time. Now I saw how the blue and yellow paintings resembled a family. Motifs flourished and faded, reduplicated and revised themselves across the seven canvases. The slender white lines in one swelled in another and then almost disappeared. Veins invisibly white. An inheritance of blue, blue paler than the young vein on an infant's forehead. And when a new blue is introduced, it makes sense.

My concentration was broken by the guard.

"Would you mind standing an arm's length away from each piece?" he said.

He was talking to two visitors. A young man and a young woman. Skinny calves, dramatic hair. In the universe of museumgoers, I recognized them; in the universe of Harwood guards, I recognized him; and if I aligned my eye with the oculus above the stools, if I peered down from the sky, even organized a high-angle shot like the one that captured Martin in 1974, gazing out from the mesa, I'd recognize myself, too, belly invisible, a woman with swimmer's shoulders peeling from the sun, in a black sleeveless dress, worrying a scrap of paper.

Looking to experiment with a simple life, Martin's art was unmotivated by nature, but she liked New Mexico for the nature; even in Taos, two minutes and you're in it. See her hugging her knees, face shielded in a round-brimmed straw hat, all in black, looking out over the abyss of canyons beyond her mesa in Cuba. You can like something and not become it, I remembered. You can be ambitious and humble, both.

The gallery felt too full with the four of us, and I felt too full with the baby. He would be getting cramped. He'd have less room to move, just when it seemed he'd need to move the most. Confinement, that archaism I'd reencountered in

Birth Project, belongs to mother and child. Perhaps it was too nineteenth century, not right or progressive or feminist or equitable enough, for me to like it the way I liked it:

A woman may be thought to be unclean after bleeding labor: confine her.

A woman may be thought too weak for socialization after labor.

A woman may be thought excessively fragile during her parturience.

A woman may be thought capable of disturbing the baby.

A woman may be torn and stretched and wearing stitches.

A woman may leak, before milk, colostrum, liquid gold.

Unable to screw for six weeks.

Exhausted, murmuring the word *morning* in her sleep.

Morning or *mourning*.

Confined to her thoughts: what can she do!

The word on her lip better than the mouth on her tit.

Talk to herself (better than hanging pictures on the walls).

(In the Cuba studio, she leaned them opposite the windows.)

To orgasm out of motherhood (unconscious convulsion).

To wish for less consent, binds, a blindfold.

Submission, renunciation, deprivation.

At one point in her long-ago life, a woman found pleasure applying watercolor to a neat square of paper towel and watching the pigment get lost in the quilting. Even more satisfying had been blotting, where an excess of color could be lifted from one's paper, leaving the impression of the brush, perhaps the idea of edges or borders, and the ghost of an intensity that's been sopped up, dialed back, the volume turned down to a hush.

I left, heady and entranced. A mute black painting.

———

One nurse brought me a giant water. Another wearing chandelier earrings rubbed an ultrasound wand on my belly: she showed us pictures, the little baby boy in Taos. I could see the foot he kept jabbing me with; it looked like a doorjamb.

After four hours, a doctor appeared; he looked like Dr. Jacoby in *Twin Peaks*. My cervix, when measured, was revealed to be quite thick. There was no indication that the mucus plug was compromised.

"Then what . . . was it?" I asked. I still wished I had taken a photo. Without evidence, the bloody mass was just another thing flushed down the toilet, decomposing in pipes, cells eking back into the earth.

"In all likelihood, discharge," the doctor said. "It's not uncommon. If you've been under any pressure . . ." He chuckled. "I know—hard to believe a pregnant woman could be under any pressure. But preterm labor would come with much more severe symptoms: contractions, leaking—severe gushing—from your vagina. A low, dull, menstrual-type cramping that persists."

I nodded. On the wall behind him, there was a poster with a cartoon baby, informing patients of the signs of preterm labor. In big letters, it read, *I'm In No Rush!* Development, I'd read three dozen times in the past few hours, happened right through the fortieth week.

"Are you going to take it easy now?" my husband asked. "Are you going to stop pushing yourself?"

I didn't answer. In the car, I read over the findings: "A single live intrauterine pregnancy is identified in the transverse position. Placenta is posterior grade 0. AFI is 11.9 cm. Fetal heart tones measure 139 bpm. Cervix appears intact on the transvaginal images and measures 4.6 cm without funneling."

I left with a hospital bracelet, a folder, a double-walled cup with a bendy straw, and instructions: Drink plenty of fluids. Stop every hour on the drive to LA and ambulate. That was the next day.

I was relieved that the baby was healthy, and I was also relieved that my blood pressure was low and my vitals were good, but, in all honesty, I was disappointed—just a little—in an admittedly teenage, drama queen way—that I hadn't gotten myself sick. How long I'd found illness validating. Attractive. The closest thing to surrealism in everyday existence.

If a child is well, or in a pathological model, normal, the child does not have EKGs or CT scans, only routine pediatric visits: checkups. By the time I was six, I had undiagnosed anxiety that manifested in a case of trichotillomania so severe I was given a pixie cut. By the time I was twelve, I'd had two surgeries: a softball-size cyst sawed from my anterior patella, another removed from my gum. Like boxcar poverty, illness became a site of romantic identification—crippled Pollyanna, with Hayley Mills's enviable ringlets!—perhaps because my mother acted most like a mother when I was sick.

When I started starving myself, I kept my hospital bracelets. Each one was a stamp in a passport booklet, a world of problems that showed I was a seasoned globetrotter. I cherished the bracelets. Kept them in my underwear drawer with a heart of rose soap. They said my name, the date, the name of a doctor, the name of a hospital: nothing of what was wrong with me. It could've been nothing or anything. It was a mystery, something to monitor or study or solve. Or, perhaps, just a mystery to observe.

Throughout high school, my mother wanted doctors to fix me. Surely, a test or a scan would reveal the extent to which my mind was corroding my body. I was starving myself then running ten miles a day then purging until the blood vessels in my eyeballs exploded: Shouldn't I be a physiological wreck? I wasn't. My weight fell and rose; my mood plunged, plummeted; my anxiety ran amok; and the EKGs and CTs were anticlimactic. Labs coded my potassium NORMAL. I sighed. Healthy, unremarkable, fine. Couldn't I keep torturing myself?

Even the discharge papers from the psych ward after my first suicide attempt offered only the flimsy instructions of therapy.

Over time, the hospital bracelets have gotten flimsier, too. Where were Martin's bands from Bellevue? Did she save them or stop, the way I did, one day just throwing the whole stash out? Did she remember anything from her fugue states?

Of all the words I looked up, *fugue* was one of the last. The psychiatric definition, applicable to Martin's biography, is second in most dictionaries. "A state or period of loss of awareness of one's identity, often coupled with flight from one's usual environment, associated with certain forms of hysteria and epilepsy." Canada, Washington, California, Oregon, New York, New Mexico, New York, Delaware, New Mexico—what if you don't have a usual environment?

A fugue is also a musical composition. A brief melody introduced by one instrument then taken up by another instrument; through the interweaving, a composition is born.

I didn't like Martin burning her old paintings. And I didn't like that I threw out my hospital bracelets, either. What would my son know from my naked wrists? All my scars had faded. Fetish is a form of hope. If I had been in the hospital, I had been somewhere, which meant I could leave, change, transform, persist. I would stay someone with something to become.

Fetal heart tone measures 139 bpm. Placenta is posterior grade 0. Here was my body in the future. I recognized that I might be drawn to myths like Martin's forever. I might forever be tempted to abandon my body, vanish into the desert, whittle life down to a series of bone-white lines.

19.

MY HUSBAND PUT HIS EAR TO my stomach while I read aloud from *Silence of the Lambs*. Clarice Starling was exploring a dead girl's closet, noticing her fat-strained shoes.

"Do you hear anything?" I said.

"I don't know." My husband hadn't shaved, and the bristles on his face poked through my dress. It was cheap, sleeveless, shapeless, black-and-white striped. I imagined the relief of discarding it, this dress and a few others like it (Old Navy size mediums; thin stretchy fabric, pilled from constant washing), and I imagined the freedom of losing the baby weight and continuing to use a wardrobe meant to last one pregnant summer: the scrappy person I could be.

"It would be about 150 beats per minute," I said. "Or 139, I guess. According to the ER sheet. *Wumpa-wumpa-wumpa-wumpa.*"

"I hear something," he said.

"I could be digesting."

He listened. I listened to him listening. Asleep on a pillow, Lucy stretched her limbs and her belly went concave. On the front patio, the neighbor lit a clove cigarette.

"Ouch! He punched me in the cheek!"

I rested my hand on the side my husband's head and traced a finger through his hair, where it started to curl. It was dark outside and bright in the room, awake with our voices, quiet in the night. A moment of contentment: the baby moving, swimming, he must've sensed it, too.

———

Before bed, I read John Cage's "Lecture on Nothing." It was our last night in the casita, and I was rousingly alert, penciling up a PDF while my husband and Lucy slept. Why had I waited so long to read this? Talk about spectacles of negation: Eighteen years ago, I'd studied Cage's 4'33" in art history. I'd never forgotten it. Not only had I never forgotten the piece, I thought about it often, in passing, the way a memory creases the flatness of a day. The auditorium of people waiting and realizing all their waiting was exactly what they'd been waiting for. When I thought about 4'33", my thoughts went from silence to Cage, whom Martin was often dismissive of. Too chancy. Too careless. Well, maybe Cage was more my speed. Whenever I heard his name, I perked up, as though hearing news of an old crush. Now that I'm done with Martin, I thought, closing my eyes, maybe I should get into Cage.

Grubby, gross realization that I'd actually thought such disloyal things the next morning. It was time to leave. My husband was in pack-up mode. I stood at my computer and paid off the last $607 of my credit card debt. I felt free and slimy. I hadn't showered after shuffling around the hospital yesterday or cooking bacon for spaghetti carbonara last night. The ultrasound jelly still coated my belly.

We showered before leaving.

"Does my body disgust you?" I asked my husband.

"No," he said, kissing me under the water. "I love your body."

Flagstaff tonight, LA tomorrow. Pull over and walk a lap around your car.

I did it once for good measure before we pulled away from the casita. Lucy was in a gash of sun on the console. The backseat was emptier now; the box of food was gone. All my Martin books were suitcased in the trunk. I felt a kind of shrill excitement, maybe or maybe not a red flag, like I had avoided something. I could go back to reading without trying to figure anything out. Cage. *A Lover's Discourse.* Sartre just to get to this quote from *Being and Nothingness*: "The lover's dream is to identify the beloved object within himself and still preserve for it its own individuality; let the Other become me without ceasing to be the other. To know [the body of the other] is to devour it yet without consuming it." There was so much more I had to devour and not consume before the baby was born.

But more importantly, there were people to see. My mother was flying out two weeks before I was due. We would go to the pier at Santa Monica and eat cacio e pepe at my favorite restaurant in Venice. My husband and I were visiting friends in Berkeley, and we would ride a hobby train through an evergreen forest. There were movies to watch, new students to meet, marketing managers to interview for case studies. I thought of one morning when my husband and I had gone hiking at El Nogal Trailhead: two coltish teenage boys ran over the footbridge, leaving all that green ash, aspen, ponderosa pine, white birch.

"I need some energy!" shouted one in a color-block windbreaker.

His friend: "At least civilization!"

I had been wrong to associate Martin so wholly with remove and solitude. Though at one point she recognized the "confusion that had to be solved" and felt she "wasn't up to the demands" of life in New York, asceticism and isolation were not facts of Martin's life. As she told Joan Simon in 1995, "I decided that human beings are herd animals. And I decided that to live properly you stay with the herd." She had, in other contexts, framed withdrawing from society as her "experiment" toward enlightenment. "I found out that what you're supposed to do is stay in the midst of life."

What an impossible hope: to find enlightenment in self-enclosure. I thought about how maybe I hadn't renounced enough. Then I thought about how, the year after making *Gabriel*, Martin moved to Galisteo. Even in 1974, when she'd attended the ICA exhibit in Philadelphia, she'd bought new clothes for the occasion and enjoyed staying in a hotel. How many times I'd thought about the lectures she'd given at colleges and universities, how she'd been an artist-in-residence in Maine, how she'd welcomed young women who pilgrimaged to see her. I thought about how, if I were left to my own devices—if I'd never had the epiphany in Detroit, if I'd never gotten pregnant—I would find stunts of silence and self-erasure satisfying for a long, long time. Perhaps all the time I was allotted. And yet, I was such an idealist, and maybe it was my greatest limitation as a writer: I believed there was so much more than the blank page.

———

In the loft at Coenties Slip, studio-slash-home, beams and fourteen-foot ceilings, claw-foot tub in the bedroom, East River, Brooklyn Bridge, each lapping wave spectacular as a nerve end, rides on tugboats and the Staten Island Ferry, between 1957 and 1967, Martin read aloud Gertrude Stein's erotic poetry and never locked her door—

One night, as Jill Johnston describes, five or six other women gathered in Martin's studio in New York, sat in a circle, almost a seance, while a storm raged outside. Martin demanded a vision, asking us all what sort of wall or body of water we imagined in our minds eye and when we saw the wall or the body of water would we cross it or could we and if so how would we do it she went right on with this exercise testing us i imagined for correct answers anyway as though nothing had happened.

What had I seen in Taos?

After writing every day for three weeks, I had 147 six-inch square text blocks. They were about Martin's writing and Martin's life and Martin's art. They were about creativity and mental illness. But mostly they were about coming to terms with who I was at this particular moment, in this particular place. The Pueblo, cheesy galleries, Dennis Hopper's grave, the cacao nibs in my yogurt, my dwindling bank account, the baby's size at twenty-seven weeks, the streams and the flowers and the trees and the elk—all of it entered these pages.

I'd looked up the definition for *picture plane*, the transparent division between the impression of space an artist creates within a painting—"fictive internal space"—and "the real space outside, in which the viewer is placed." I wondered if a part of me was caught in that division. I also wondered what made the internal space of the painting fictive. And why the space in which the viewer existed was real. *Tundra* had been real; I had been a fiction before it.

Before coming to Taos, I'd finished writing a manuscript of poems called *New Life*. I was thinking about the baby as the new life. Yet, as I prepared to leave, I wondered if that new life were mine. Perhaps all along, through Martin, I'd been trying to see my own life anew.

———

To see things anew, you must do things anew. Two years later, I will. Two years later, I'll take a train to Chicago. I'll exit on Adams and walk east toward La Salle. I'll find a sky-scraper associated with the School of the Art Institute of Chi-cago and take the elevator to the fourteenth floor. November, Tuesday before Thanksgiving. I'll leave my family to be in a room with the lights off, listening to Agnes Martin talk.

There are DVDs of two interviews with Martin con-ducted by Kate Horsfield and Lyn Blumenthal: one from 1974 in New Mexico, another from 1976. I watch each interview twice, reading along with a printout of the transcript, adding back in Martin's *ehs* and *you sees*, noting when she laughs, when she looks down at her lap, when she stares out the win-dow or wipes her mouth with a handkerchief. Are her eyes cagey or concentrated? Is she purposefully evasive or exact-ing? How should I read her voice pitching up? Why have I never read that someone defaced one of her paintings with an ice cream cone?

In the first interview, she's asked about her writing. "I don't write at all," Martin says. "These are old now, years old."

(And yet, on timelines, the years between 1967 and '74 are often cited as a time when she was writing. Did she not write? Did she not want to be writing?)

With a pencil, I sketch her wearing her apron in her rocking chair, the window on her left. Next to the sketch, I write, "a laugh in her voice."

A camera jerks when she describes infancy as the state when people are their most perceptive: "Very young children can play in the dirt with a stick, without boredom, from early morning until lunch . . . But if you played in the dirt with a stick, you wouldn't last that long. But he is perceiving and responding all the time, and satisfied, which means that his response is keener than ours. And then we lose it for a while, because we have so many other things on our minds."

What I'm not expecting is her likening maternal instinct to artistic inspiration in 1976. So impassioned that she leans away, back into the rocking chair, Martin says of the artist recognizing inspiration through moments of clarity: "it's just like the mother knows that she has to take care of the infant or die . . . She'd do anything. She would die for that child . . . some mothers at least. And we, too, we know we have to do it."

Finally, I stand up. The Video Data Bank director has an old green accordion folder for me. He's photocopied everything inside. He lets me take the file into the viewing room and tells me I can take pictures of anything I want.

I open the folder and my heart lifts in my chest: a pair of close-up portraits of Martin stare up at me. No. I am not important. What is important is the unedited transcript, cloudy with carbon. The veering in Martin's speech. A few grand conspiracies. Why, for instance, are we talking about the deaths of Marilyn Monroe or Jackson Pollock or Garland? Who is the *they* that have killed them?

Writing is all a trick anyway, I think. I'm so protective of my romantic delusions. And Martin's writing—which was frequently transcribed by friends. No, she doesn't like biography, she says, in a bit of transcript from footage that wasn't included on the DVDs. She says biography is all about the writer's point of view. "Depending on how romantically minded the person was that wrote the biography, you see, it could just be a pack of lies! According to that person's point of view."

I try not to be romantically minded. I try to hold the mysteries. And yet, whenever I think I have grown skeptical, whenever I think I can see her as a person (not a woman, a doorknob), whenever I think I've heard enough of her weaving together Eastern philosophy and American Transcendentalism and Judeo-Christian allusions (those Ezekiel Dry Bones I need to look up), whenever I think I know that she was a person who pawed at her mouth and fidgeted with squares of tissue, I read the text and become entranced.

A few times recently my therapist has had to tell me, "Just because you're a mother doesn't mean you ever stop longing for a mother. Ever."

Leaving the viewing room, I feel very quiet and very uncomfortable with the quiet. Martin's voice is in my ear, and I see her everywhere. The grids of windows in the buildings, the pocked rectangles of concrete forming the sidewalk. The scar across my bikini line has begun to itch. I acknowledge my sympathies to domineering fatalists. Martin may not have titled her own paintings, but she sharpened her own pencils.

———

While my husband was hauling suitcases from the casita, I called my mother. I wanted to let her know I was okay. When I reassured her that I was totally fine, she told me about her new aqua class. The restaurant she went to with my dad. A person writing a cringey memoir in her workshop.

And yet, having come out of yesterday's scare unscathed, I felt patient. I hadn't ruined my body. I hadn't hurt the baby. I'd take care of myself these last couple months; I'd be generous with my family and my friends and my husband; I'd have a big heart so I could be a good mother.

So this was where Martin and I parted. Johnston described Martin's basic approach to life as "nothing happens. no verticals. everything the same. a quiet existence. not much time for other people's problems. solitude and loneliness and contentment with one's self. the union of opposites without trying to do so."

How was I going to be a writer with "nothing happens"?

And why had I put so much stock in Martin's "basic approach"? I was haunted by an interview with Mary Fuller (McChesney). Fuller had met Martin in New Mexico in 1950, when Martin was going by Aggie, and her memory of young Aggie was colored by ambition, Martin saying things like, "I'm going to make it . . . I don't care who I have to fuck or how I have to do it." Fuller was not the only person who noted Martin's drinking. Her ambivalence. Who suggested Martin was "re-writing [her] whole history."

In the future, I needed to remember: if contact with my mother had made me foggily matrophobic, I could simply read Martin's canvases. Sometimes she let the texture show through (*The Desert* [1965]) and sometimes she smoothed the surface (*The Harvest* [1965]). A painting needn't lose its tooth.

"We're all set," I said to my mom, as my husband closed the trunk. "I'll let you know when we're back in LA."

"I'm glad this time was so rejuvenating for you, honey," she said.

I hated that—as though I'd gone on an *Eat, Pray, Love* in New Mexico. But I said, yeah, it really was, and I love you.

Our car crunched over the gravel as we backed away from the casita. We turned onto Weimer and then we were driving past the bowling alley and the cloverleaf, past the Sonic where we'd gotten ice cream, past the turnoff to Dennis Hopper's grave, and soon we'd left the Cristobal de la Serna Land Grant. A pair of signs: ROSE GARDEN. LABYRINTH. I wore sunglasses and held my mouth firm. I didn't want to cry.

"What do you think you'll take away with you from this time?" my husband asked.

I paused, looking at the scrubby cactuses and rock faces blurring by, the line of pines in the distance. I didn't want it to end. That's why she strained to make a permanent painting, I thought. She loved this so much, too.

"I don't know," I said. "What about you?"

"The simplicity," my husband said. "I want to live like

we lived in the casita. Even when we have the baby. Do you think that's possible?"

"Of course," I said. I paused. "I think maybe fear is useful. I was so afraid, and I wouldn't have written one-hundred-and-whatever pages otherwise." I thought of something a novelist once told me—that what you wrote should matter, because you were going to die someday. Knowing the baby was going to be born reminded me of that truth, and now I could see beauty more acutely. "If I have to do it again, now I know that I can. She just kept making art. In some ways, that's the most inspiring thing about Martin."

At mile marker 36, I noticed a white Mercedes passing alongside us. It was snub-nosed, candied with dust, boxy and gorgeous, the first white Mercedes I'd seen in weeks. It was going fast. A white blaze, all alone. Speeding toward Taos.

I wanted to tell my husband how Martin had loved a Mercedes; I would've, even if I was repeating myself, but he was explaining how this time, these seventeen days, had changed him, too. I looked over my shoulder. The car was gone. I turned and stared at everything passing by. The Rio Grande Gorge. The mesa right now. All up and down the road, there were crosses, names and snapshots peeking out from pink and blue flowers in the wind.

Postscript

*The intensity of her touch is what made it beautiful.
And in the end, it's what makes any beautiful art
beautiful. It's the intensity of what is put into it.*

—Pat Steir on friend Agnes
Martin's paintings

MARTIN EVERYWHERE AND NOWHERE.

"Perhaps she was a transitional object," an older friend said. "She served her purpose."

A Thursday in October, 8:33 a.m.: Needle in the spine: I hunched over the back of a swivel chair, hugged it, and wailed. I was on a metal table, hair tucked in a blue cloth cap, a partition separating me from the doctor and his assistants. I didn't hear anything. I didn't feel anything. My husband saw my organs—I only tasted them, a sick tang in the back of my mouth, an unctuous bottled smell that made me wince. Muscat yellow light. Keep breathing, you're doing great, someone said. Then there was the baby, hair matted wet, pert doll nose, two tiny fists. And finally, everything changed.

After so long trying to practice Martin's path to inspiration, here I was, hit with what I had to do: it was time to be a mother.

———

Sometimes I try to draw like Agnes Martin. My son has his sketchbook open on the rug. There's a yellow hatbox of crayons and oil pastels. He's two. We're lying on our stomachs on the living room floor, surrounded by blocks and books. Often, I take Martin's parenting advice—I let him play alone, hoping he'll develop a sensibility.

He has. He likes mango, croissants, tomatoes, and "lil cookie." He likes, on a walk, crouching at landscaping stones, choosing one, and handing it to me or my husband. "*Aaah*," he says, expectantly. "Thank you so much," I say. When he's ready to move on, I replace the rock. He likes Talking Heads' "Psycho Killer." He likes when I pause, reading to him, and let him finish sentences. He likes when I read the dedication.

He likes when I recite books. I've memorized *Madeline*, *Perfect Pets*, *Cookie's Week*, and *My First Counting Book*. Many children's books are about identifying with the strangest characters (especially *Mr. Rabbit and the Lovely Present*, where a limber rabbit suggests to a pinafored little girl she give her mother red underwear for her birthday), and yet it was a book without characters—*My First Counting Book* by Lillian Moore, pictures by Garth Williams—that shook me.

One through ten, you count animals. One puppy, two lambs, four kittens, a rabbit's five cabbages. The number eight begins, "Swish, swish." Eight fish swim in the brook; eight fish are wise to swim past the hook. "Swish, swish." When my son says it, it sounds like "shh, shh." When he's sitting at the dinner table, when he's grinning on his changing pad, that's my cue.

One morning, my son and I were hanging out in my office. He was taking chapbooks off the bookshelf. *Agnes Martin: Paintings, Writings, Remembrances* was laid out on the daybed. I was skimming through the list of works, looking for a pattern in the titles. In *Painting, Writings, Remembrances*, Martin's works on paper are a coda to the paintings. "Blue Hitchcock," my son said—I knew which book he had found. I was reading through titles when I stopped. *Eight Fish Under Water*, from 1963, ink on paper, ten inches by ten inches.

I heard a voice in my office: "Swish, swish."

I flipped to the piece. Against a background of division signs, running horizontal across the page, there were eight ovals (two columns of four). The ovals were only outlines. Without the title, it would've been easy to see them as eyes. Or canoes. Or female genitalia.

"Look at this," I said to my son, dropping to the ground. I held up the book. "Do you see one-two-three-four-five-six-seven-eight fish?"

"Shhh, shhh," he said.

He ran out of the room, and I followed him. Later, though, I turned to the Slip photograph I loved so much: Martin on the slant of the roof, Youngerman and Indiana and Seyrig— and the little boy, Youngerman and Seyrig's son, Duncan, age two. His hair was straighter, lighter than my son's, and his face was rounder, sturdier. I looked at him. I looked at Martin. *Swish, swish.* She was beaming.

———

It doesn't matter how lightly I apply the crayon. If I use *Good Night, Gorilla* as a straight edge. My straight line isn't Martin's. My straight line rarely stays elegant and simple. I draw two straight lines and clutter it. A diagonal appears. A string of dots. My Martinesque drawings—amidst my son's circles and houses and curlicues and furtive squares—look like experiments, little swatches testing out a pattern, the logic for which I'm still unsure.

There's no time to fret my busy mind. My son turns the page. Today every composition gets a fuchsia backward six. If I start devoting myself to any drawing—a right-facing seal, a left-facing penguin—I'm thwarted. The page turns.

There are no unwritten pages in this sketchbook or the other nine in the house. My son fills them, revisits each page, adds a line, scribbles, concentrates on a corner, moves on.

I love watching him draw. Sometimes, lying on the rug with him, I can smell the milky sweetness of his skin, warmed by the sunlight spilling through the windows. Our faces are close. His golden hair flops in his eyes. His feet talk to each other. The tip of his oil pastel is flat. The paper needs to be peeled. It doesn't bother him. Little bothers him. No cutting out tags from his clothes.

I feel it more powerfully than anything in my life: We are so happy. That was his first sentence. One morning I found him standing in his crib, grinning across the room at a pink toy piano and the stuffed sheep. "I'm so happy!" he crowed. "I'm so happy today!"

In Taos, I took out my colored pencils. I still have a good set because, until college, I still took art classes. I still believed I could forget people praised my writing and replace my notebook with a sketchbook. I still believed that, in my next life, I would be an artist. Not a past life (Martin once told Lizzie Borden that in a past or imagined life she could've been a cannibal). No, I kicked my heart into the future.

That is no longer a thought. My heart is on the rug.

I even bought a sketchbook—a cheap one for kids near the pipe cleaner kits at an office supply shop. The massive pad my son uses is from the art supply store. But in Taos, I never tried to draw like Martin. This was an oversight. *Eight Fish Under Water*, it was right there, a size I could manage. No color to perfect. No perfect circles. Just division sign, repeat, division sign, repeat. Cover the page. The inky black pen I wrote with would work; it would have been a good place to begin imitation. Eight empty eyes.

I wasn't taking things head-on Taos, not really.

I drew a mango.

I craved mango. Now my son loves it. Now we eat mango together.

"He sure loves mango mongo," my mother says, when she visits.

Often, with my hand by my son's, our wrists brushing, I close my eyes to stop the tears. Happy tears, I tell my son, if he sees. He's too young to ask what is wrong. Someday, I hope he'll believe me when I say "nothing."

I try another set of lines. Salmon-pink bars alternating

with lemon-yellow ribbons. Straight, blurry, beautiful. Finally, my gentle colors shimmer. Finally, there's a felicity to the difference in width.

Then my son moves my hand and draws a big circle with brick-red oil pastel. Three smaller circles inside it. A cat. He takes my hand. He puts it on the paper. He says, "Please draw a cat."

So I do.

Acknowledgments

I am grateful to the generous women who spoke with me about Agnes Martin. Suzanne Hudson, for "all of the all" and everything. Lizzie Borden shared memories and photos from her visit to mesa, guiding me to important insights with her singular brilliance. Ann Wilson provided crucial context about Agnes's years at Coenties Slip. Pat Steir and Kim Treiber gave me a glimpse into their friendship with Agnes. Dani at Another Gaze gave me an early peek at an important issue.

Tom and the staff at Video Data Bank brought Agnes's voice into a cloudy Tuesday.

To my first art teachers—Dianne Washburn and Pat Page: You showed me the world comes alive through art.

To Donald, for the postcard fourteen years ago.

When this project was a grain of sand in the metaphorical desert, the Center for Academic Innovation and Creativity at Mount Saint Mary's University supported my ideas and plans. Many thanks to my Mount friends and colleagues, past and present: Bob Perrins, Kim Middleton, Johnny Payne, Wendy McCredie, Leonard Schulze, and Marcos McPeek-Villatoro.

The team at Catapult has given me the space to grow as an essayist and memoirist. Thank you to: Jonathan Lee, for believing in this manuscript and seeing its potential in many largely unwritten pages; Megha Majumdar, for your brilliant eye for structure and organization; Alicia Kroell, for shepherding the book into being. Ryan Quinn, for the astute copyedits.

Thanks to Markus Hoffmann and Grace Ross for believing in my writing.

My friends in sentences, from the classroom and beyond: Kathleen, Maggie, Geoff, David, Ottessa, Cyrus, Andrew, Mel, Margaret, Erin, Antonia, Natania, and Cameron. To Monica and Barbara, always. Special, eternal gratitude for the eleventh-hour nonfiction encouragement from Seth, Lucas, and Melissa. Amanda, thank you for giving me the faith.

To Aubyn and Al, for the joy.

To my parents, for their unflagging support, and to my sister for her example. To my brother, in pursuit of eudaimonia.

To Lucy, helper, nurse, yaourt ride-or-die.

To Thomas, for being my partner on these roads. Every day you inspire me with your tirelessness, your commitment, your heart.

To N, for sharing your unwritten pages.

And, of course, to Agnes.

Bibliography

Abrams, Matthew Jeffrey. "Meeting Gabriel." *Affidavit*, April 9, 2019. www.affidavit.art/articles/meeting-gabriel/.

Agnes Martin: The Distillation of Color. New York: Pace Publishing, 2022.

Attiyeh, Jenny. "Agnes Martin: An Artist on Her Own." *Horsefly*, 2001. www.scribd.com/doc/221427944/Interview-with-Taos -artist-Agnes-Martin.

Baker, J. A. *The Peregrine*. London: William Collins, 2017.

Berger, John. *Permanent Red: Essays in Seeing*. London: Writers and Readers Publishing Cooperative, 1960.

Berger, John, writer. "Ways of Seeing, Episode 1," directed by Michael Dibb. Aired January 8, 1972, in broadcast syndication. Accessed at www.youtube.com/watch?v=0pDE4VX_9Kk.

Borden, Lizzie. "Agnes & Perfection." *Another Gaze*, March 21, 2022. www.anothergaze.com/agnes-martin-lizzie-borden/.

Borden, Lizzie. Interview with author. February 19, 2022.

Brennan, Kathleen and Jina Brenneman, directors. *Agnes Martin: Before the Grid*. Brennan Studio, 2018. Fifty-six minutes. www.kanopy.com/en/product/475566.

Buren, Daniel and Thomas Repensek. "The Function of the Studio." *October*, vol. 10 (1979): 51–58. doi.org/10.2307/778628.

D'Agata, John, ed. *The Making of the American Essay*. Minneapolis: Graywolf Press, 2016.

Dillard, Annie. "The Deer at Providencia." In *Teaching a Stone to Talk*. New York: Harper Perennial, 2013.

Eisler, Benita. "Life Lines." *The New Yorker,* vol. 68 (1993): 70. www.newyorker.com/magazine/1993/01/25/life-lines.

Freud, Sigmund. *Beyond the Pleasure Principle,* edited by Ernest Jones. London: International Psycho-Analytical Press, 1942. www.libraryofsocialscience.com/assets/pdf/freud_beyond_ the_pleasure_principle.pdf.

Freud, Sigmund. *The Standard Edition of the Complete Psychological Works of Sigmund Freud.* Translated by James Strachey. London: Hogarth, 1953.

Glimcher, Arne. *Agnes Martin: Paintings, Writings, Remembrances.* London: Phaidon, 2012.

Gruen, John. "Agnes Martin: 'Everything, everything is about feeling . . . feeling and recognition." *ARTnews,* September 1976. www.artnews.com/art-news/retrospective/what-we -make-is-what-we-feel-agnes-martin-on-her-meditative -practice-in-1976-4630/.

Hudson, Suzanne. *Agnes Martin: Night Sea.* London: Afterall Books, 2016.

Hudson, Suzanne. "Agnes Martin, On a Clear Day." In *Agnes Martin,* edited by Lynne Cooke, Karen Kelly, and Barbara Schröder, 118–131. New York: Dia Art Foundation, 2014.

Johnston, Jill. "Agnes Martin: Surrender and Solitude." *Village Voice,* September 13, 1973. www.scribd.com/doc/312092133 /Jill-Johnston-Agnes-Martin-Surrender-and-Solitude.

Kandel, Eric. *The Disordered Mind: What Unusual Brains Tell Us About Ourselves.* New York: Farrar, Straus and Giroux, 2018.

Keats, John. "Ode on a Grecian Urn." Poetry Foundation. www .poetryfoundation.org/poems/44477ode-on-a-grecian -urn.

Lance, Mary, director. *Agnes Martin: With My Back to the World.* New Deal Films, 2002. Fifty-seven minutes. vimeo.com/on demand/withmybacktotheworld/351017628.

Lippard, Lucy. *From the Center: Feminist Essays on Women's Art.* New York: E. P. Dutton & Co. Inc., 1976.

Mansoor, Jaleh. "Self-Effacement, Self-Inscription." In *Agnes Martin,* edited by Lynne Cooke, Karen Kelly, and Barbara Schröder, 154–169. New York: Dia Art Foundation, 2014.

Martin, Agnes. Video Data Bank interviews.

Martin, Agnes. Letter to Samuel Wagstaff. Smithsonian Archive. www.aaa.si.edu/collections/samuel-j-wagstaff-papers-6939 /subseries-1-1/box-2-folder-11.

"Martin, Agnes." Union List of Artist Names Online. Getty. vocab.getty.edu/page/ulan/500024489.

McChesney, Mary Fuller. "Oral history interview with Mary Fuller McChesney, 1994 Sept. 28." Interview by Susan Landauer. Archives of American Art. www.aaa.si.edu/collections/ interviews/oral-history-interview-mary-fuller-mcchesney-12498.

Michelson, Annette. "Agnes Martin: Recent Paintings." *ArtForum,* January 1967. www.artforum.com/print/196701 /agnes-martin-recent-paintings-36776.

Morris, Frances and Tiffany Bell, editors. *Agnes Martin.* London: Tate, 2015.

Nochlin, Linda. "Why Have There Been No Great Women Artists?" www.writing.upenn.edu/library/Nochlin-Linda_ Why-Have-There-Been-No-Great-Women-Artists.pdf.

"Picture Plane." London: The National Gallery. www.national gallery.org.uk/paintings/glossary/picture-plane.

Prendeville, Brendan. "The Meanings of Acts: Agnes Martin and the Making of Americans." *Oxford Art Journal,* vol. 31, no. 1, Oxford University Press, 2008, 51–73. doi.org/10.1093/oxartj /kcm027.

Princenthal, Nancy. *Agnes Martin: Her Life and Art.* London: Thames & Hudson, 2016. "reproduction, n." OED Online, Oxford University Press, December 2021. www.oed.com /view/Entry/163102. Accessed March 3, 2022.

Sandler, Irving. "AGNES MARTIN." *Art Monthly,* no. 169, 1993, 3–11.

Schwarz, Dieter, editor. *Agnes Martin: Writings.* Ostfildern-Ruit: Cantz Verlag, 1991.

Simon, Joan. "Perfection Is in the Mind: An Interview with Agnes Martin." *Art in America,* May 1996.

Steir, Pat. Interview with author. March 2, 2022.

Suzuki, Shunryū. *Zen Mind, Beginner's Mind: Informal Talks on Zen Meditation and Practice.* Boston: Shambhala, 2011.

Treiber, Kim. Interview with author. February 25, 2022.

Wilson, Ann. Interview with author. February 11, 2022.

Wilson, Ann. "Oral history interview with Ann Wilson, 2009 April 19-2010 July 12." Interview by Jonathan Katz. Archives of American Art. www.aaa.si.edu/collections/interviews/oral-history-interview-ann-wilson-15968.

Zell, Ethan, Amy Beth Warriner, and Dolores Albarracín. "Splitting of the Mind: When the *You* I Talk to Is Me and Needs Commands." *Social Psychology and Personality Science,* vol. 3, issue 5, December 1, 2011. doi.org/10.1177/1948550611430164.

JOANNA NOVAK's short story collection, *Meaningful Work*, won the Ronald Sukenick Innovative Fiction Contest. She is also the author of three books of poetry, most recently *New Life*, and a novel, *I Must Have You*. Her work has appeared in *The New Yorker*, *The Paris Review*, *The New York Times*, and other publications. She is a co-founder of the literary journal and chapbook publisher *Tammy*.